RÔTIS

A big thankyou to Fred for the *p'tits déj-rôtis* from 7.45 am ...
Thanks to Sandramahu ... So, have you made up your mind?
Thanks to Amarylis for even roasting on Sundays ... It was worth it!
Thanks to Alexandre for roasting on Monday, from midnight, for a
whole night ... definitely deserving of a little Saint-Joseph!
Emmanuel ... Champion of the world!

For my friend Nicoco, without whom all this pleasure would not be possible!

Stéphane

Stéphane Reynaud

RÔTIS

**Roasts for every
day of the week**

Photography by Frédéric Lucano

Illustrations

MURDOCH BOOKS

Lundi
C'EST RÔTI
DE BŒUF

Monday
is roast beef

Wednesday
is roast chicken and game

Mercredi
C'EST RÔTI
DE VOLAILLE

jeudi
C'EST RÔTI
DE COCHON

Thursday
is roast pork

Mardi
C'EST RÔTI
DE VEAU

Tuesday
is roast veal

Vendredi
POISSON EN RÔTI

Friday
is roast fish

Samedi
ÇA RÔTIT POUR DE
L' AGNEAU

Saturday
is roast lamb

Dimanche MIDI
TROP DE LA CHANCE
C'EST RÔTI DE
GIBIER

Sunday lunch
is roast game

Et avec tout ça?
(GARNITURES ET ACCOMPAGNEMENTS)

And with all this?
vegetables and side dishes

Dimanche SOIR
IL EN RESTE

Sunday evening
is all the rest

1

Cut a strip of barding fat the length
of the roast.
Wrap this strip around the roast.

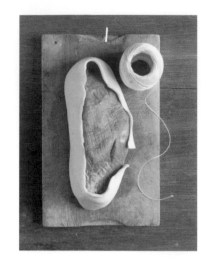

2

Tie a piece of string lengthways
around the roast to secure the fat.

HOW TO TIE
A BEEF ROAST

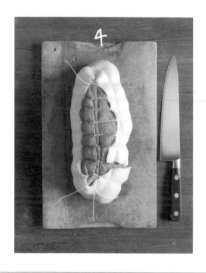

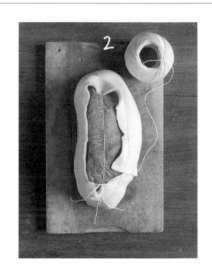

4

Continue the process of wrapping
and tying until you reach the end of
the roast. Finish with two loops on
top of one another then tie a knot.

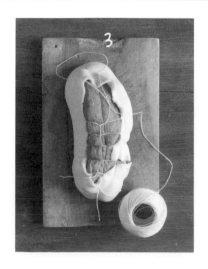

3

Tie the string very tightly around
one end of the roast and make
a knot. Lay the string along the
length of the roast. Place your
thumb on the string 2 cm from
the top knot. Hold your thumb
down firmly, then wrap the other
end of the string around the roast.
Allow the string to pass under
your thumb, then pull the string
upwards to tighten the hold.

1

Take a chicken, a good knife and some kitchen string. Remove the innards of the chicken and set it down so that the breast is facing you.

2

Tie the string around the neck skin and the wings, then tuck these underneath the chicken.

4

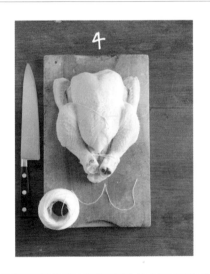

HOW TO TIE
A CHICKEN

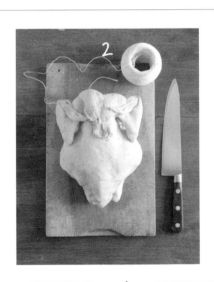

4

Wrap the string around the wings several times, pull the string tight, then tie a knot.

3

Pass the string over the breast, slip it under the thighs and wrap it around the end of the drumsticks. Take the string back to the upper wings.

Lundi
C'EST RÔTI
DE BŒUF

Monday
is roast beef

A tender roast

For a tender roast, the piece of beef eye fillet must be properly aged when you buy it. Be careful that the meat isn't too fresh, otherwise it is liable to be too tough.

It is very important when the roast is done to allow it to rest for a few minutes, covered with a sheet of foil. This will let the flesh relax and the juices that are locked in during cooking can redistribute throughout the meat.

LEFT

Rare

In a rare roast, all of its juices stay in the middle. The cooking time is longer, so the temperature in the middle is higher. The rare roast is a little firmer to the touch than the very rare roast and its juice is more pink.

BELOW

HOW WOULD YOU LIKE

YOUR ROAST
BEEF COOKED?

Very rare ('blue')

For the carnivore par excellence, the 'very rare' roast should be extremely well caramelised on all sides from cooking on a high heat. The roast is seared to keep its juices inside, and the temperature in the middle is just lukewarm. The roast should be very soft to the touch and its juice very red.

ABOVE

Medium

A roast beef cooked medium is still pink in the middle. It is firm to the touch and its juice is very clear. This level of roasting can make the meat a little dry.

LEFT

Rôti de bœuf en cocotte d'oignons

ROAST BEEF ON A BED OF ONIONS

1.25 kg (2 lb 12 oz) beef eye fillet
2 tablespoons olive oil
200 ml (7 fl oz) white wine
6 large onions, peeled and quartered
1 tablespoon brown sugar
2 bay leaves
50 g (1 ¾ oz) butter

Preheat the oven to 200°C (400°F/Gas 6).

Heat the olive oil in a flameproof casserole dish. Add
the beef and brown on all sides over high heat.

Remove the beef from the dish and set it aside on a large plate.

Deglaze the casserole dish with the white wine and scrape the
bottom of the dish well using a spatula. Add the onions, sugar
and bay leaves and cook, covered, until the onions are soft.

Return the beef to the casserole dish. Add the butter,
cover, and roast in the oven for 25 minutes.

Remove the roast from the oven and allow the beef to rest
in its juices, covered, for 10 minutes, before serving.

| SERVES 6 | PREPARATION TIME 15 minutes | COOKING TIME 30 minutes |

Rôti de nos mamies
GRANDMA'S ROAST BEEF

1.25 kg (2 lb 12 oz) beef eye fillet
2 tablespoons olive oil
600 g (1 lb 5 oz) kipfler potatoes, halved
6 carrots, sliced into rounds
4 French shallots, peeled and halved
6 garlic cloves
a few thyme sprigs
1 bay leaf
100 g (3½ oz) butter
200 ml (7 fl oz) white wine

Preheat the oven to 180°C (350°F/Gas 4).

Heat the olive oil in a large frying pan
that has a lid. Add the potato, carrot,
shallot and garlic cloves, and sauté over
medium heat. Add the thyme and bay leaf,
cover, then cook, stirring regularly, for
15 minutes. Season with salt and pepper.

Heat 50 g (1¾ oz) of the butter in
a flameproof roasting tin. Add the
beef and brown on all sides over
high heat. Transfer to the oven and
roast the beef for 20 minutes.

Remove the roast from the oven and
allow the beef to rest in its juices,
covered with foil, for 10 minutes.
Don't turn the oven off.

Transfer the roast onto a carving board.

Deglaze the roasting tin with white
wine, scraping the bottom of the
tin well, then mix in the remaining
butter into the juices to a smooth
and creamy consistency. Add the
vegetables to the roasting tin, then
return to the oven to cook for 5 minutes,
before serving with the roast.

Rôti de bœuf façon bortsch
BORSCHT-STYLE ROAST BEEF

1.25 kg (2 lb 12 oz) beef eye fillet
½ savoy cabbage, finely diced
1 celery stalk, diced
4 carrots, diced
2 tablespoons olive oil
100 g (3½ oz) diced smoked bacon
4 French shallots, peeled and halved
200 ml (7 fl oz) vegetable stock
4 medium cooked beetroot (beets)
   (*see p. 136*), diced
50 g (1¾ oz) butter
1 small bunch parsley, chopped
1 small bunch dill, chopped
100 g (3½ oz) crème fraîche

Preheat the oven to 180°C (350°F/Gas 4).

Blanch the cabbage and celery in
boiling salted water and refresh them
immediately. Cook the carrot until firm.

Heat the olive oil in a flameproof roasting
tin. Add the beef and brown on all sides
over high heat. Transfer to the oven and
roast the beef for 10 minutes, then
remove and add the bacon and shallot.
Return to the oven and roast for a further
10 minutes.

Remove the roast from the oven and
allow the beef to rest in its juices,
covered with foil, for 10 minutes. Then
transfer the roast onto a carving board.

Deglaze the roasting tin with the
vegetable stock. Add the beetroot,
carrot, cabbage and celery and cook
on the stovetop over medium heat for
10 minutes. Add the butter, season with
salt and pepper and sprinkle with
chopped parsley.

Mix the dill with the crème fraîche,
season with salt and pepper, and
serve on the side.

SERVES 6
PREPARATION TIME
20 minutes
COOKING TIME
25 minutes

SERVES 6
PREPARATION TIME
20 minutes
COOKING TIME
30 minutes

Rôti de bœuf à la ficelle

POACHED BEEF ROAST

1.25 kg (2 lb 12 oz) beef eye fillet
2 tablespoons olive oil
3 onions, peeled and roughly sliced
200 ml (7 fl oz) white wine
6 leeks, halved lengthways
6 turnips, peeled and halved
6 pontiac potatoes, peeled and halved
3 sweet potatoes, peeled and halved

GRIBICHE SAUCE
6 cornichons, finely chopped
1 French shallot, peeled and finely chopped
1 teaspoon capers
100 g (3½ oz) mayonnaise
juice of 1 lemon

Heat the olive oil in a flameproof casserole pot. Add the onion
and brown over high heat. Deglaze with the white wine and add
2 litres (70 fl oz/8 cups) of water. Add the leek and turnip, and
cook for 40 minutes.

Next, add the pontiac and sweet potatoes and cook for a further
20 minutes. Season with salt and pepper.

Tie the beef with kitchen string at 2 cm (¾ inch) intervals, then tie
the beef to the opposite ends of a wooden spoon, so that the spoon
can be balanced over the top of the pot and the beef will be
submerged into the hot stock. Poach for 10 minutes, making sure
that the beef does not touch the sides of the pot.

Remove the casserole pot from the heat and transfer the beef onto
a carving board. Cover with foil and allow to rest for 5 minutes.

To make the gribiche sauce, combine the cornichon, shallot and
capers in a bowl. Stir in the mayonnaise, then add the lemon juice
and combine well.

Slice the beef very thinly and cover with vegetables and stock.
Serve with the gribiche sauce and sea salt on the side.

| SERVES 6 | PREPARATION TIME
45 minutes | COOKING TIME
1 hour 10 minutes |

Bordelaise sauce

Peel and finely chop 4 onions. Cook
the onion in 500 ml (17 fl oz/2 cups)
of good red wine over medium heat,
and allow to reduce until it thickens.
Add the onion-wine mixture to the
roasting tin. Add 50 g (1¾ oz) of
butter and stir well until the butter
is completely combined. Season
with salt and pepper.

Saint-Marcellin sauce

Melt 2 mature Saint-Marcellin
cheeses in 30 ml (1 fl oz) of cream in
a small saucepan over medium heat.
Reduce until the sauce thickens,
then add a pinch of nutmeg.

4 SAUCES

TO GO WITH BEEF

Béarnaise sauce

Peel and finely chop 2 French
shallots and 1 small bunch of
tarragon, then cook in 100 ml
(3½ fl oz) of wine vinegar over
medium heat until the liquid has
completely evaporated. Turn down
to a very low heat and add 2 egg
yolks, then whisk vigorously to a
creamy texture. Add 200 g (7 oz) of
melted butter, little by little, to the
egg mixture, beating constantly.
Season with salt and pepper.

Shallot butter

Peel and finely chop 2 French
shallots and finely chop 1 small
bunch of chives. Dice 150 g (5½ oz)
of butter into cubes, and leave at
room temperature. Combine the
butter, chives and shallot well.
Season with fine sea salt and
freshly ground black pepper.

Filet de bœuf rôti en croûte de champignons
ROAST FILLET OF BEEF WITH MUSHROOMS 'EN CROÛTE'

1.25 kg (2 lb 12 oz) piece of beef eye fillet
2 tablespoons olive oil
50 g (1¾ oz) butter
300 g (10½ oz) button mushrooms, quartered
150 g (5½ oz) cep mushrooms, quartered
3 French shallots, peeled and finely chopped
1 small bunch parsley
2 slices sandwich bread, roughly torn in pieces
300 g (10½ oz) ready-made puff pastry
1 egg yolk

Preheat the oven to 160°C (315°F/Gas 2–3).

Heat the olive oil in a flameproof casserole dish.
Add the beef fillet and brown on all sides over high heat
for 7 minutes, then remove from the dish and allow the
beef to cool on a rack. Season with salt and pepper.

Heat the butter in a frying pan and sauté the mushrooms
and shallot over medium heat, until all the water has
been released.

Put the mushroom and shallot mixture with the parsley
and bread into a food processor, and process to a fine
stuffing mixture. Season with salt and pepper.

Spread the mushroom stuffing along the length of the fillet.

Roll out the puff pastry to a length that will completely wrap
around the beef fillet. Brush the edges of the pastry with egg yolk,
then lay the beef fillet on the pastry and wrap it up tightly like a
parcel, pressing the seams together firmly and tucking the ends
under. Put the parcel seam-side down into the casserole dish, then
brush all over with the remaining egg yolk.

Make a couple of vents in the pastry to allow steam to escape, then
bake in the oven for 20 minutes.

| SERVES 6 | PREPARATION TIME 45 minutes | COOKING TIME 30 minutes |

Côte de bœuf au gros sel
RIB ROAST WITH COARSE SALT

2 x 1 kg (2 lb 4 oz) pieces of beef eye rib
6 large baking potatoes
6 marrow bones
½ bunch chives, finely chopped
50 g (1 ¾ oz) butter
sea salt, to serve

CHIVE BUTTER
100 g (3½ oz) butter, at room temperature
2 French shallots, peeled and finely chopped
½ bunch chives, finely chopped

Preheat the oven to 180°C (350°F/Gas 4).

Wrap the potatoes in foil and bake in the oven for about 45 minutes.
Test to see if they're done by inserting the point of a knife.

Bring a large saucepan of water to the boil. Add the marrow
bones, return to the boil, then simmer over a medium heat for
15 minutes or until the centre of the bones is soft. Drain the bones,
then season with coarse salt and garnish tops with chives.

Meanwhile, heat the butter in a flameproof roasting tin. Add the
beef ribs and brown them on each side until well caramelised.
Transfer to the oven and roast the ribs for 5 minutes.

To make the chive butter, combine the butter, shallot and
chives in a bowl and mix well. Season with salt and pepper.
Split open the potatoes and top with the chive butter.

Slice the beef ribs into thick slices, sprinkle with sea
salt and serve with the marrow bones and potatoes.

| SERVES 6 | PREPARATION TIME
5 minutes | COOKING TIME
45 minutes |

Rosbif aux olives vertes
ROAST BEEF WITH GREEN OLIVES

1.25 kg (2 lb 12 oz) beef eye fillet
1 bunch sorrel
100 ml (3½ fl oz) olive oil, plus
    extra 4 tablespoons
6 French shallots, peeled and
    roughly sliced
6 garlic cloves
6 ripe tomatoes, cut into wedges
100 g (3½ oz/⅔ cup) green olives, pitted
50 g (1¾ oz/⅓ cup) pine nuts
100 g (3½ oz) feta cheese, cut
    into small cubes

Preheat the oven to 180°C (350°F/Gas 4).

Blanch the sorrel in boiling salted water, refresh it immediately, then strain well. Process the sorrel and olive oil in a food processor. Season with salt and pepper.

Heat 2 tablespoons of the extra olive oil in a frying pan. Add the shallot and cook over medium heat until softened. Add the garlic, tomato, olives and pine nuts. Combine well and allow the mixture to stew for about 10 minutes. Season with salt and pepper.

Heat the remaining olive oil in a flameproof roasting tin. Add the beef and brown on all sides over high heat. Transfer to the oven and roast the beef for 10 minutes, then remove and add the tomato mixture and scatter over feta. Return to the oven and roast for a further 10 minutes.

Remove the roast from the oven and allow the beef to rest in its juices, covered with foil, for 10 minutes.

Drizzle over the sorrel oil before serving.

Rosbif au vin de Fleurie
ROAST BEEF WITH FLEURIE WINE

1.25 kg (2 lb 12 oz) beef eye fillet
1 litre (35 fl oz/4 cups) Fleurie
    wine, or light-bodied fruity
    red, such as Pinot Noir
1 tablespoon honey
1 teaspoon mixed spice
100 ml (3½ fl oz) crème de cassis
6 conference pears, peeled
6 French shallots, peeled
2 tablespoons olive oil
50 g (1¾ oz) butter

Preheat the oven to 180°C (350°F/Gas 4).

Put the Fleurie wine, honey, mixed spice and crème de cassis in a large saucepan and bring to the boil. Immerse the pears and shallot in the mixture, and cook for about 30 minutes: the pears should remain firm. Remove the pears and the shallots and reduce the wine mixture by one-third.

Heat the olive oil in a flameproof casserole dish. Add the beef and brown on all sides over medium heat, until the beef is well caramelised. Transfer to the oven and roast the beef for 20 minutes.

Remove the roast from the oven and allow the beef to rest in its juices, covered, for 10 minutes. Then transfer the roast onto a carving board.

Deglaze the casserole dish with the wine sauce. Stir in the butter and season with salt and pepper. Add the pears and shallots and reheat them in the sauce.

Carve the beef into thick slices and return to the casserole dish to serve.

SERVES 6
PREPARATION TIME 15 minutes
COOKING TIME 20 minutes

SERVES 6
PREPARATION TIME 30 minutes
COOKING TIME 1 hour

Filet de bœuf piqué d'ail aux escargots
GARLIC-STUDDED FILLET OF BEEF WITH ESCARGOT

1.25 kg (2 lb 12 oz) beef eye fillet
10 garlic cloves, 5 halved and 5 chopped into chips
80 g (2¾ oz) butter
1 tablespoon walnut oil
100 ml (3½ fl oz) white wine
4 dozen snails
4 French shallots, peeled and roughly chopped
1 small bunch parsley, chopped
50 ml (1¾ fl oz) pastis
2 tablespoons olive oil

Stud the fillet with the garlic halves.

Heat the butter in a flameproof casserole dish with walnut oil.
Add the fillet and brown on all sides over high heat. Transfer to
the oven and roast the beef for 20 minutes. Remove the beef
from the oven, cover with foil and allow to rest in its own juices
for 10 minutes.

Deglaze the dish with the white wine. Add the snails, shallot
and parsley and combine. Allow the snail mixture to reduce for
10 minutes, then add the pastis and flambé the whole dish.

Heat the olive oil in a frying pan, add the garlic chips
and sauté until golden. Add the garlic mixture to
the snails, and season with salt and pepper.

Carve the fillet into thin slices and scatter over some of the
snails and garlic mixture. Serve the rest on the side.

| SERVES 6 | PREPARATION TIME
20 minutes | COOKING TIME
35 minutes |

eMardi
C'EST RÔTI
DE VEAU

Tuesday
is roast veal

Rôti de veau tout simplement

ROAST VEAL, PLAIN AND SIMPLE

1 kg (2 lb 4 oz) veal fillet
2 tablespoons olive oil
300 ml (10½ fl oz) white wine
6 French shallots, peeled
6 garlic cloves, unpeeled
6 carrots, peeled and sliced
6 potatoes, peeled and cut into wedges
2 swedes (rutabaga), peeled and cut into wedges
2 bay leaves
a few thyme sprigs
50 g (1¾ oz) butter

Heat the olive oil in a flameproof casserole dish. Add
the veal fillet and brown over high heat until it is well
caramelised. Cover and allow to cook for 10 minutes on low
heat, adding a little white wine from time to time. Add the
shallots and garlic, then cook for a further 10 minutes.

Add the carrot, potato, swede, bay leaves and thyme and
combine well. Add the rest of the white wine and a little
water if necessary, and continue cooking for 30 minutes over
low heat, making sure that the vegetables don't stick.

Add the butter, cover, and cook for a further 10 minutes.
Season with salt and pepper. Allow the roast to rest in its juices,
covered, for 10 minutes before serving.

| SERVES 6 | PREPARATION TIME
20 minutes | COOKING TIME
1 hour |

Rôti de veau retour des Indes

ROAST VEAL WITH AN INDIAN ACCENT

1.25 kg (2 lb 12 oz) veal fillet
1 teaspoon ground cinnamon
1 teaspoon curry powder
1 teaspoon ground cumin
2 tablespoons olive oil
6 garlic cloves, chopped
3 French shallots, peeled and chopped
50 g (1¾ oz) fresh ginger, chopped
6 bulb spring onions (scallions) and stems
3 lemongrass stems
50 g (1¾ oz/⅓ cup) almonds, peeled
20 g (¾ oz) pine nuts
150 g (5½ oz) dried apricots

Combine the cinnamon, curry powder and cumin in a shallow bowl and mix well. Rub the spice mixture all over the veal fillet.

Heat the olive oil in a flameproof casserole dish. Add the veal fillet and brown over high heat with the garlic, shallot and ginger.

Halve the bulb spring onions and chop the stems. Split the stems of the lemongrass lengthways. Arrange the onions and stems, lemongrass, almonds, pine nuts and apricots around the veal. Add 500 ml (17 fl oz/2 cups) of water, cover, and cook over low heat for 1 hour 30 minutes. Season with salt and pepper.

Rôti de veau au caramel

CARAMEL ROAST VEAL

1.25 kg (2 lb 12 oz) veal fillet
200 ml (7 fl oz) Sauternes
1 stick licorice root
2 tablespoons brown sugar
80 g (2¾ oz) butter
1 small bunch coriander (cilantro), finely chopped
100 g (3½ oz) peanuts, roughly crushed

The day before, put the Sauternes, licorice root and brown sugar in a saucepan and bring to the boil. Remove and set aside to cool, then place in the refrigerator and allow to infuse overnight.

The next day, heat the butter in a flameproof casserole dish. Add the veal fillet and brown over high heat. Cover and cook over low heat for 1 hour 30 minutes, basting regularly with a little water. Season with salt and pepper.

Preheat the oven to 180°C (350°F/Gas 4).

Mix together the coriander and peanuts. Moisten the roast with a little Sauternes, then cover with the coriander-peanut mixture. Pour over the licorice-flavoured sauce. Roast in the oven for 30 minutes, until the veal forms a lovely caramelised crust. Serve immediately.

SERVES 6	SERVES 6
PREPARATION TIME 20 minutes	PREPARATION TIME - RESTING TIME 10 minutes - 12 hours
COOKING TIME 1 hour 40 minutes	COOKING TIME 2 hours

Rôti de veau au citron confit
ROAST VEAL WITH PRESERVED LEMON

1.25 kg (2 lb 12 oz) veal fillet
zest of 1 lemon
2 tablespoons olive oil
2 French shallots, peeled and thinly sliced
200 ml (7 fl oz) white wine
3 zucchini (courgettes), sliced
1 preserved lemon, cut into 6 wedges
200 g (7 oz) cherry truss tomatoes on the vine
100 g (3½ oz) dry-salted black olives
a few lemon thyme sprigs
50 g (1¾ oz) butter

Preheat the oven to 150°C (300°F/Gas 2).

Rub the lemon zest over the veal fillet.

Heat the olive oil in a flameproof roasting tin. Add the
veal fillet and caramelise on all sides over high heat.
Add the shallot, then roast in the oven for 1 hour, basting
regularly with the white wine.

Remove the roast and arrange the zucchini, lemon wedges,
cherry tomatoes and black olives around the meat, then
scatter with the thyme sprigs. Return to the oven for a further
15 minutes, then add the butter. Season with salt and pepper.

| SERVES 6 | PREPARATION TIME
20 minutes | COOKING TIME
1 hour 15 minutes |

Rôti de veau aux olives

ROAST VEAL WITH OLIVES

1.25 kg (2 lb 12 oz) veal fillet
4 tablespoons olive oil
10 sage leaves
1 bay leaf
200 ml (7 fl oz) white wine
3 onions, peeled and chopped
3 tomatoes
8 garlic cloves, thinly sliced
100 g (3½ oz) green olives, pitted and sliced
a few thyme sprigs
a few rosemary sprigs

Preheat the oven to 160°C (315°F/Gas 2–3).

Heat 2 tablespoons of the olive oil in a flameproof roasting tin.
Add the veal fillet and brown over high heat until it caramelises.
Add the sage leaves and bay leaf, then roast the veal in the oven
for 1 hour 30 minutes, basting it regularly with a little white wine.

Heat the remaining olive oil in a frying pan and sauté the
onion over medium heat until quite soft. Set aside.

Cut a small cross in the base of each tomato, then plunge the
tomatoes into a saucepan of salted boiling water for 5 seconds.
Drain, remove the skins and dice the flesh. Set aside.

Remove the roast from the oven and transfer to a serving dish.

Put the garlic and green olives in the roasting tin and sauté
in the juices over medium heat on the stovetop. Add the
tomato and caramelised onion and cook for 5 minutes. Season
with salt and pepper. Pour the vegetable mixture over the
roast, add a few thyme and rosemary sprigs, then serve.

| SERVES 6 | PREPARATION TIME
20 minutes | COOKING TIME
2 hours |

Collier de veau, compotée de tomates
NECK OF VEAL WITH STEWED TOMATOES

1.25 kg (2 lb 12 oz) neck of veal
6 very ripe tomatoes
2 tablespoons olive oil
100 ml (3½ fl oz) olive oil
8 onions, peeled and sliced
300 ml (10½ fl oz) white wine
50 g (1¾ oz) tomato sauce (ketchup)
20 g (¾ oz) brown sugar
1 tablespoon veal glaze

Cut a small cross in the base of each tomato. Plunge the
tomatoes into a saucepan of salted boiling water for
15 seconds. Drain, remove the skins, then cut into wedges.

Heat 2 tablespoons of olive oil in a flameproof casserole dish.
Add the veal neck and brown on all sides over high heat. Cover
and cook over low heat for 30 minutes, turning regularly.

Next, add the olive oil and onion, and allow the onion to
caramelise. Add the tomato, then stew for 30 minutes, uncovered.

Add the white wine, tomato sauce, brown sugar and veal
glaze. Season with salt and pepper, cover, and cook for 1 hour
on low heat, making sure that the tomato doesn't stick.

Remove from the heat, and allow the veal to rest in its
juices, covered, for 10 minutes before serving.

| SERVES 6 | PREPARATION TIME
15 minutes | COOKING TIME
2 hours |

Fennel

In a flameproof casserole dish, cook 1 veal shank in 2 litres (70 fl oz/ 8 cups) of meat stock over medium heat for 1 hr 45 mins. Drain veal from stock and transfer to a baking dish. Mix 3 tablespoons of honey with 3 tablespoons of soy sauce. Brush half the glaze over the shank. Sprinkle with fennel seeds, then roast in the oven at 180°C (350°F/ Gas 7) for 20 mins until the shank is caramelised, regularly covering the shank with the remaining glaze.

Osso buco style

In a large saucepan, cook 1 veal shank in 2 litres (70 fl oz/8 cups) of stock over medium heat for 1 hr 30 mins. Arrange 800 g (1¾ lb) of sliced tomatoes, 6 onions and 10 sliced garlic cloves in a flameproof casserole dish. Add 2 bay leaves and 200 ml (7 fl oz) of white wine, then bake in the oven at 200°C (400°F/Gas 6) for 1 hr. Lay the shank in the middle of the stewed tomato mixture and return to the oven for a further 30 mins at 180°C, making sure it is well covered with tomatoes.

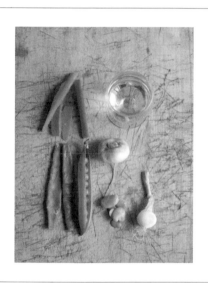

4 IDEAS

FOR SERVING
VEAL SHANK

Spring vegetables

In a large saucepan, cook 1 veal shank in 2 litres (70 fl oz/8 cups) of water with 2 leeks and 1 bouquet of garni over medium heat for 1 hr 30 mins. Remove the bones. Heat 2 tablespoons of olive oil in a flameproof casserole dish, and sauté over medium heat 6 carrots, diced, 3 bulb spring onions, halved, 2 baby turnips, chopped, 500 g (1 lb 2 oz) of peas and 200 g (7 oz) of broad beans. Add 300 ml (10½ fl oz) of veal stock and the boned veal shank, then cook in the oven at 180°C (350°F/Gas 4) for 30 mins, basting the meat in its own juices.

Chanterelle mushrooms

In a flameproof casserole dish, cook 1 veal shank in 2 litres (70 fl oz/ 8 cups) of meat stock over medium heat for 1 hr 45 mins. Drain the veal from the stock and return the veal to the dish. Surround the veal with 1 kg (2¼ lb) of chanterelle mushrooms, 300 g (10½ oz) of diced smoked bacon, 6 unpeeled garlic cloves and 2 rosemary sprigs. Drizzle over a little olive oil and bake in the oven at 160°C (315°F/ Gas 2–3) for 30 mins.

Carré de veau rôti au poivre
ROAST RACK OF VEAL
WITH PEPPER

1 rack of veal with 6 ribs
100 g (3½ oz) butter
200 ml (7 fl oz) white wine
1 tablespoon green peppercorns
3 onions, peeled and halved
a few thyme sprigs

Use a skewer (or the point of a knife) to pierce the rack of veal and insert the green peppercorns.

Preheat the oven to 180°C (350°F/Gas 4).

Heat 50 g (1¾ oz) of butter in a flameproof roasting tin. Add the veal rack and brown over high heat. Baste the rack with a little white wine, add the onion and thyme, then roast in the oven for 1 hour, basting the veal regularly.

Remove the roast from the oven and transfer the veal rack onto a serving plate and allow it to rest for 10 minutes. Meanwhile, reduce the cooking juices over medium heat with the remaining butter. Season with salt and pepper.

Quasi au lard fumé
VEAL RUMP WITH
SMOKY BACON

1.25 kg (2 lb 12 oz) veal rump
100 g (3½ oz) butter
4 garlic cloves
1 end-slice prosciutto with rind, finely diced
2 bay leaves
12 French shallots, peeled
6 thick slices smoked bacon
150 ml (5 fl oz) white wine

Heat 50 g (1¾ oz) of butter in a large flameproof casserole dish. Add the veal rump and brown on all sides over high heat.

Add the garlic cloves, prosciutto and bay leaves. Season with salt and pepper. Cover and cook on low heat for 1 hour 30 minutes, basting regularly with a little water if necessary.

Add the shallot and bacon, then cover and cook for a further 30 minutes.

Transfer the rump, shallot and bacon onto a serving plate and place near an opened heated oven.

Remove the garlic cloves and crush them to extract the pulp. Combine the garlic pulp with the meat juices and deglaze with white wine. Reduce, then stir in the remaining butter. Serve the veal rump drizzled with the garlic-flavoured juices and prosciutto.

SERVES 6	SERVES 6
PREPARATION TIME 10 minutes	PREPARATION TIME 15 minutes
COOKING TIME 1 hour	COOKING TIME 2 hours

Poitrine de veau roulée
ROLLED VEAL BREAST

1.5 kg (3lb 5 oz) veal breast*
2 tablespoons coriander seeds
1 tablespoon chilli powder
1 tablespoon mixed herbs
2 tablespoons olive oil
2 yellow capsicums (peppers)
2 red capsicums (peppers)
2 green capsicums (peppers)

Preheat the oven to 120°C (250°F/Gas ½).

Combine the coriander seeds, chilli powder and mixed herbs in a shallow bowl with some salt and pepper. Sprinkle the veal breast with the seasoning.

Roll and tie the veal breast at 2 cm (¾ in) intervals with kitchen string. Place in a good size roasting tin and drizzle with olive oil. Roast the veal for 4 hours in the oven, turning regularly. Use a skewer or trussing needle to check how the meat is cooking: the skewer should easily enter the meat.

Remove the roast and arrange the whole capsicums around the meat. Return to the oven for a further 30 minutes, or until wilted.

Remove the roast from the oven and allow it to rest in its juices, covered with foil, for 10 minutes before serving.

*Ask your butcher to bone a veal breast and trim some of the fat.

SERVES 6	PREPARATION TIME 15 minutes	COOKING TIME 4 hours 30 minutes

Mercredi C'EST RÔTI DE VOLAILLE

Wednesday
is roast chicken and game

Poulet tout simplement
CHICKEN, PLAIN AND SIMPLE

1 large free-range chicken
2 tablespoons olive oil
sea salt
6 garlic cloves, unpeeled
6 onions, unpeeled
6 potatoes, skin on and cut into wedges

Preheat the oven to 180°C (350°F/Gas 4).

Wipe the chicken and pat dry with kitchen paper.

To tie the chicken, fold the wings back and tuck them
underneath the chicken, then tie the legs together with string.

Brush the chicken with olive oil and sprinkle with coarse
sea salt. Place the chicken in a flameproof roasting
tin, then arrange the garlic cloves and onions around
it. Roast the chicken in the oven for 1 hour.

Remove the roast and arrange the potato wedges around
the chicken. Baste the chicken with some of its cooking
juices, then return to the oven for another 30 minutes.

Serve the chicken covered with its cooking juices, with the
garlic, onions and potatoes.

| SERVES 6 | PREPARATION TIME
5 minutes | COOKING TIME
1 hour 30 minutes |

Boursin

This is a complicated process consisting of carefully unwrapping a Boursin cheese and stuffing it into the chicken. At serving time, mix the Boursin that has melted during cooking with the cooking juices.

Tomatoes

Peel and chop 2 French shallots. Heat 2 tablespoons of olive oil in a frying pan, and sauté 250 g (9 oz) of cherry tomatoes over medium heat, until their skins split. Add the shallot and allow the mixture to stew together.

Next, add 1 tablespoon of tomato sauce (ketchup), 1 tablespoon of soy sauce and 1 teaspoon of tarragon mustard. Combine well, then use the mixture to stuff the chicken.

4 IDEAS

FOR STUFFING CHICKEN

Tarragon

Finely chop the leaves of 1 bunch of tarragon and mix with 200 g (7 oz) of crème fraîche. Finely chop 2 bulbs of spring onions (scallions), including stems, and add to the tarragon cream. Season with salt and pepper, then use the mixture to stuff the chicken.

Goat's cheese

Strip the leaves from 1 bunch of mint and finely chop. Crush a fresh Saint-Maure-de-Touraine cheese, add 3 tablespoons of olive oil, the chopped mint leaves, salt and pepper, and combine well. Use this mixture to stuff the chicken.

Spices

Combine 100 ml (3½ fl oz) of olive oil with 1 teaspoon each of curry powder, paprika, mixed herbs, cumin and fine sea salt. Carefully separate the skin from the flesh of the chicken via the neck opening, without breaking it. Lubricate the flesh with the spiced olive oil.

Marjoram–ginger

Peel 50 g (1¾ oz) of fresh ginger, and process it in a food processor with 100 ml (3½ fl oz) of olive oil and a little coarse salt. Separate the skin from the flesh of the chicken via the neck opening, without breaking it. Lubricate the inside with the gingered olive oil and slip in a few marjoram leaves. Place the chicken in the refrigerator for 1 hour before cooking.

More !
4 IDEAS
FOR STUFFING CHICKEN
... under the skin !

Truffle

Slice 10 g (¼ oz) of truffle into thin slivers. Carefully separate the skin from the flesh of the chicken via the neck opening, without breaking it. Lubricate the flesh with olive oil, add a little coarse salt, then lay truffle slices all over the flesh. Wrap the chicken in plastic wrap and allow it to rest in the refrigerator for 24 hours before cooking. If you wish, you can use the less expensive (less intensely perfumed) summer truffles and replace the olive oil with truffle oil.

Coriander

Process 1 bunch of coriander (cilantro), 1 teaspoon of sea salt, 2 garlic cloves and 100 ml (3½ fl oz) of olive oil in a food processor until well blended. Carefully separate the skin from the flesh of the chicken via the neck opening, without breaking it, then massage the flesh with the coriander mixture.

Poulet rôti aux anchois et au romarin
ROAST CHICKEN WITH ANCHOVIES AND ROSEMARY

1 large free-range chicken
12 anchovies in oil, halved
12 garlic cloves, halved
2 branches rosemary, broken into small sprigs
1 small bunch tarragon, leaves only
3 French shallots, peeled and chopped
3 tablespoons crème fraîche
2 tablespoons olive oil

Prepare the chicken the day before. Use the pointed end of a knife to pierce the chicken in several places. Then insert the anchovy, garlic clove and rosemary sprig in each opening. Cover with plastic wrap and place in the refrigerator overnight.

The next day, combine the tarragon leaves, shallot and crème fraîche in a bowl and mix through well. Remove the chicken from the refrigerator and stuff the chicken with the tarragon mixture.

Preheat the oven to 180°C (350°F/Gas 4).

Tie the chicken, then put it in a flameproof roasting tin. Drizzle the olive oil over the chicken, then roast for 1 hour and 30 minutes in the oven.

Carve the chicken into portions and serve with the stuffing on the side.

Note: Be careful with seasoning as the anchovies already contain a lot of salt.

| SERVES 6 | PREPARATION – RESTING TIME
20 minutes – overnight | COOKING TIME
1 hour 30 minutes |

Cuisses de poulet rôties et farce de fruits secs

ROAST CHICKEN THIGHS WITH FRUIT AND NUT STUFFING

6 chicken Maryland leg quarters, with skin on
10 g (¼ oz) dried cep mushrooms
4 tablespoons olive oil, plus extra
2 French shallots, peeled and finely chopped
150 g (5½ oz) chicken breast fillet, chopped
150 g (5 fl oz) cream
6 dates, chopped
6 dried apricots, chopped
50 g (¾ oz/⅓ cup) hazelnuts
10 chives, chopped
6 thin slices prosciutto
2 red capsicums (peppers), sliced
2 green capsicums (peppers), sliced
300 g (10½ oz) cherry tomatoes

Bone the chicken Maryland leg quarters, retaining the
leg bone and as much of the flesh as possible.

Rehydrate the dried mushrooms in boiling water, then drain.

Heat 2 tablespoons of olive oil in a frying pan. Add the shallot
and cook until softened, then add the mushrooms and cook for
5 minutes.

Put the chicken breast, cream, dates, apricot, hazelnuts, chives
and mushroom mixture in a food processor. Blend until
combined ingredients form a smooth stuffing mixture.
Season with salt and pepper.

Preheat the oven to 180°C (350°F/Gas 4).

Stuff each chicken thigh with the stuffing mixture, then wrap
a slice of prosciutto around the thigh and tie with string.

Heat 2 tablespoons of olive oil in a flameproof roasting tin. Add
the capsicum and brown over medium heat. Remove from the
heat. Drizzle generously with a little more olive oil, then lay
the chicken thighs on top. Bake for 35 minutes in the oven.

Remove from the oven and add the cherry tomatoes and
return to the oven to roast for a further 10 minutes.

| SERVES 6 | PREPARATION TIME 45 minutes | COOKING TIME 45 minutes |

Pigeons rôtis aux petits légumes

ROAST PIGEONS WITH MIXED VEGETABLES

3 large pigeons*
150 g (5½ oz) butter
50 ml (1¾ fl oz) armagnac
4 potatoes, peeled and diced
3 carrots, peeled and diced
1 fennel bulb, peeled and diced
4 French shallots, peeled and finely sliced
150 ml (5 fl oz) ruby or tawny port
1 tablespoon honey
1 rosemary sprig
sea salt

Heat the butter, 50 g (1¾ oz) for each pigeon, in a large
flameproof casserole dish. Brown the pigeons one
at a time over high heat until well caramelised.

Set the pigeons aside and in the same casserole dish
add the giblets and flambé with the armagnac.

Add the potato, carrot, fennel and shallot to the casserole dish
and sauté for 5 minutes. Add the port, honey and rosemary sprig.
Cover and cook for a further 5 minutes over medium-low heat.

Arrange the pigeons on the bed of vegetables, cover, then cook
for 10 minutes over low heat. Season with sea salt, then allow
the pigeons to rest in their juices, covered, for 5 minutes
before serving.

*Ask your butcher to gut and clean the pigeons, reserving the giblets.

| SERVES 6 | PREPARATION TIME
20 minutes | COOKING TIME
20 minutes |

Magrets farcis aux cèpes et au foie gras
DUCK MAGRETS STUFFED WITH CEP MUSHROOMS AND FOIE GRAS

4 duck magrets
3 tablespoons honey
2 tablespoons soy sauce
50 ml (1¾ fl oz) cognac
1 teaspoon ground cinnamon
50 g (1¾ oz) butter
200 g (7 oz) cep mushrooms, diced
3 French shallots, peeled
and finely chopped
200 g (7 oz) foie gras

Prepare the ducks the day before. Use the pointed end of a sharp knife and slash the skin of the duck magrets in a lattice pattern through to the flesh.

Mix the honey and soy sauce together in a saucepan. Add the cognac and cinnamon, combine well and bring to the boil.

Arrange the magrets in a casserole dish and drizzle over the honey marinade. Cover and put in the refrigerator for 24 hours. Turn the magrets over from time to time so that the marinade is distributed evenly.

The next day, heat the butter in a frying pan and sauté the mushroom and shallot over medium heat. Season with salt and pepper.

Slice the foie gras into long bars. Cut a pocket lengthways into the magrets and stuff with some of the foie gras bars. Place 2 magrets skin-side down and cover with mushrooms, then top each with a second magret skin-side up, then tie up with string.

Cook the magrets in a heavy-based frying pan over medium heat for 7 minutes on each side: the fat in the skin should melt and the flesh should stay red.

Slice the bands of string before serving.

Dinde rôtie en farce fine
ROAST TURKEY WITH RICH FORCEMEAT

1 quality free-range turkey*
50 g (1¾ oz) sultanas
50 ml (1¾ fl oz) armagnac
300 g (10½ oz) chicken
breast fillet, chopped
150 g (5½ oz) foie gras, diced
4 slices prosciutto, sliced into thin strips
3 French shallots, peeled and chopped
1 bunch curly-leaf parsley, chopped
200 ml (7 fl oz) cream
12 thin slices smoked streaky bacon

Plump up the sultanas in a bowl of hot water, drain, then add the armagnac.

Preheat the oven to 160°C (315°F/ Gas 2–3).

Put the turkey giblets, chicken breast, foie gras, prosciutto strips, shallot, parsley, sultanas and cream in a food processor. Blend until the combined ingredients form a smooth stuffing mixture. Season with salt and pepper.

Lay the turkey out flat. Stuff the turkey, making sure it retains its shape. Wrap slices of bacon around the turkey, then tie up tightly with string.

Put the turkey in a large flameproof roasting tin and roast in the oven for 1 hour 30 minutes.

Remove the roast and allow the turkey to rest in its juices, covered with foil, for 10 minutes before serving.

Ask your butcher to clean the inside of the turkey, then bone it via the back, taking care not to damage the flesh. Retain the giblets and only the bones of the upper wings.

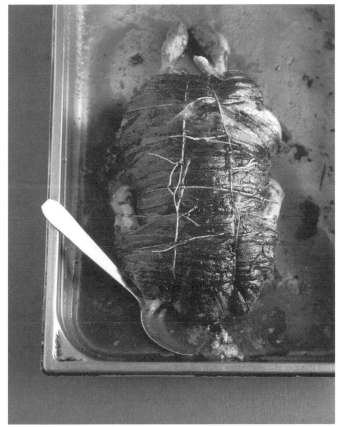

SERVES 6
PREPARATION TIME - MARINATING TIME 45 minutes - 24 hours
COOKING TIME 15 minutes

SERVES 6
PREPARATION TIME 45 minutes
COOKING TIME 1 hour 30 minutes

Pintade rôtie au chou

ROAST GUINEA FOWL WITH CABBAGE

1 guinea fowl
1 savoy cabbage
100 g (3½ oz) butter
200 g (7 oz) piece smoked streaky bacon, diced
3 Toulouse sausages, sliced
6 garlic cloves
4 onions, peeled
160 ml (5¼ fl oz) white wine

Preheat the oven to 200°C (400°F/Gas 6).

Separate the cabbage leaves by removing the central rib.
Cook the leaves in a large saucepan of boiling salted water.

Heat the butter in a flameproof casserole dish. Add the
guinea fowl and brown on both sides over high heat,
then roast, uncovered in the oven for 30 minutes.

Transfer the dish onto the stovetop. Add the bacon,
sausage, garlic and onions, and brown over low
heat. Add the cabbage, then the white wine.

Reduce the oven temperature to 160°C (315°F/Gas 2–3).
Cover the casserole dish and return to the oven for 1 hour,
checking regularly that the cabbage isn't sticking. Season with salt
and pepper before serving.

| SERVES 6 | PREPARATION TIME
20 minutes | COOKING TIME
1 hour 30 minutes |

Canard entier aux dragées

WHOLE ROAST DUCK WITH SUGARED ALMONDS

1 Muscovy duck
4 French shallots, peeled and chopped
1 tablespoon rosemary leaves
2 teaspoons thyme
150 g (5½ oz) sugared almonds, roughly chopped
2 tablespoons honey

Preheat the oven to 160°C (315°F/Gas 2 –3).

To make the stuffing, combine well the shallot, rosemary and thyme, and stuff the duck.

Mix the almond and honey together, then rub the mixture all over the duck.

Put the duck in a large flameproof roasting tin and roast in the oven for 45 minutes (for a duck that's still pink).

Remove the duck from the oven and portion it. If the thighs are a little firm, cook them for a further 15 minutes.

Transfer the duck pieces, well-covered with the honeyed almond mixture, onto a baking tray. Grill for 5 minutes to caramelise the dish.

| SERVES 6 | PREPARATION TIME
10 minutes | COOKING TIME
45 minutes |

Italian flat beans and chorizo

Chop 150 g (5½ oz) of spicy chorizo sausage into thin strips. Slice 400 g (14 oz) of flat beans and cook in boiling salted water. Peel and slice 3 red onions. Arrange all of the ingredients around the duckling after 15 mins of cooking. Deglaze with white wine then return to the oven for 15 mins at 160°C (315°F/Gas 2–3).

Grapes

Arrange 200 g (7 oz) of white seedless grapes and 200 g (7 oz) of red seedless grapes around the duckling after 15 mins of cooking, then return to the oven for 15 mins at 160°C (315°F/Gas 2–3). Remove the roasting tin from the oven, deglaze with muscat, then reduce over low heat. Add 50 g (1¾ oz) of butter and mix well.

4 IDEAS

FOR SERVING
DUCKLING

Orange

Juice 2 oranges. Peel and zest a third orange, then remove the pith and slice into segments. Reduce 100 ml (3½ fl oz) of wine vinegar until completely evaporated, then add the orange juice, zest and 50 g (1¾ oz) of brown sugar. Let the sugar dissolve. Coat the duckling with the mixture after 15 mins of cooking, then return to the oven for another 15 mins at 160°C (315°F/Gas 2–3), basting the duckling in its juices. Serve with orange segments.

Tomatoes and green olives

Thinly slice 6 garlic cloves. Roughly chop 600 g (1 lb 5 oz) of tomatoes. Heat 2 tablespoons of olive oil in a flameproof casserole dish and brown the duckling, then remove and set aside. Add the tomato and garlic to the dish and sauté. Add 2 thyme sprigs, 200 g (7 oz) of pitted green olives and 1 tablespoon of plain flour and allow the mixture to stew. Lay the duckling on the vegetables, cover, and cook for 20 mins over medium heat.

Rôti de lapin en rognonnade
ROLLED ROAST RABBIT WITH KIDNEYS

3 saddles of rabbit
4 tablespoons olive oil
9 garlic cloves, 1 crushed and 8 unpeeled
4 rabbit kidneys
6 sage leaves, finely chopped
2 teaspoons rosemary leaves
600 g (1 lb 5 oz) kipfler potatoes
6 rabbit livers, roughly chopped

Heat 2 tablespoons of olive oil in a frying pan. Add the crushed
garlic and sauté over medium heat, then remove from the
heat and allow the mixture to infuse for 10 minutes.

Bone the saddles of rabbit via the belly, taking
care not to separate the two fillets.

Lay the saddles out flat, flesh-side up. Brush the rabbit flesh
with the garlic mixture and season with salt and pepper.

Arrange 4 rabbit kidneys lengthways along each saddle,
scatter with sage and rosemary, then close up the saddles
and tie with kitchen string at 2 cm (¾ in) intervals.

Heat the remaining olive oil in a flameproof casserole dish.
Brown the rabbit saddles, one at a time, over high heat, turning
regularly. Add more oil if necessary as you brown each saddle.

Return all the rabbit saddles to the casserole dish. Arrange the
potato, rabbit livers and garlic cloves around the saddles. Season
with salt and pepper, cover, and cook over low heat for
30 minutes, turning the rabbit and potatoes regularly.

SERVES 6	PREPARATION TIME	COOKING TIME
	30 minutes	30 minutes

Lapin rôti à la lyonnaise
LYONNAISE-STYLE ROAST RABBIT

1 large rabbit*
60 ml (2 fl oz/¼ cup) olive oil
6 onions, peeled and sliced
6 thick slices smoked streaky bacon, diced
6 tomatoes, cut into wedges
1 rosemary sprig
3 bay leaves
500 ml (17 fl oz/2 cups) white wine

Preheat the oven to 180°C (350°F/Gas 4).

Roughly chop the rabbit liver and set aside.

Heat half the olive oil in a flameproof casserole dish.
Add the rabbit portions and brown over high heat,
then remove from the dish and set aside.

Add the remaining oil, onion and bacon to the dish, then
cook over medium heat until well caramelised. Return the
rabbit to the dish. Add the tomato, rosemary, bay leaves
and liver. Deglaze with the white wine and season with salt
and pepper. Cover and roast in the oven for 1 hour.

Remove the rabbit portions and set aside. Return the casserole
dish to the oven and stew the tomato for a further 20 minutes.
Return the rabbit portions to the dish, arranging them on top
of the mixture, and cook, covered, for 10 minutes to reheat.

Ask your butcher to portion the rabbit, saving the liver.

| SERVES 6 | PREPARATION TIME
15 minutes | COOKING TIME
1 hour 30 minutes |

jeudi
C'EST RÔTI
DE COCHON

Thursday
is roast pork

Cochon rôti tout simplement
ROAST PORK, PLAIN AND SIMPLE

1 deboned pork leg
100 ml (3½ fl oz) olive oil
200 ml (7 fl oz) white wine
3 French shallots, unpeeled
1 bulb garlic, unpeeled
sea salt

Preheat the oven to 150°C (300°F/Gas 2).

Heat the olive oil in a flameproof roasting tin. Add the pork
and seal the roast on all sides over medium heat. Transfer to
the oven and roast for 45 minutes, making sure to baste the
roast regularly with white wine and a little water, if necessary.

Remove the roast and add the shallots and garlic. Return to
the oven and roast for a further 45 minutes, basting the roast
regularly, so that the cooking juices take on the flavour of the
garlic and shallots.

Season with the sea salt and pepper before serving.

| SERVES 6 | PREPARATION TIME
5 minutes | COOKING TIME
1 hour 30 minutes |

Carré de cochon en croûte de sel

RACK OF PORK IN A SALT CRUST

1 rack of pork with 6 ribs
2 garlic cloves
3 French shallots, peeled and roughly chopped
100 ml (3½ fl oz) olive oil
100 ml (3½ fl oz) soy sauce
5 lemongrass stems, finely chopped
3 kg (6 lb 12 oz) coarse salt
300 ml (10½ fl oz) white wine
1 small bunch tarragon

The day before, put the garlic, shallot, olive oil and
soy sauce in a food processor. Blend until all ingredients
are combined into a marinade mixture. Combine the
lemongrass with the blended mixture.

Use the point of a knife to pierce the roast all over.
With a basting brush, completely cover the rack of pork
in marinade, then cover in plastic wrap. Put the pork in
the refrigerator for at least 24 hours.

The next day, preheat the oven to 160°C (315°F/Gas 2–3).

Moisten the salt with the white wine.

Put the rack of pork in a flameproof casserole dish. Scatter
the tarragon over the pork, then cover it completely with the
coarse salt (the pork should be entirely invisible). Roast in
the oven for 1 hour 45 minutes.

When ready to serve, place the roast on the dinner table and
break the salt crust, so that the cooking aromas fill the room.

| SERVES 6 | PREPARATION - RESTING TIME
30 minutes - 24 hours | COOKING TIME
1 hour 45 minutes |

Asparagus and smoky bacon

Cook 1 bunch of green asparagus in a large quantity of boiling salted water, keeping them firm. Cut them in two, then roll each half in a slice of bacon. Roast the rack of pork for 1 hour at 160°C (315°F/Gas 2–3). Arrange the asparagus around the rack at the end of cooking. Add 50 g (1¾ oz) of butter, then return to the oven for another 10 mins.

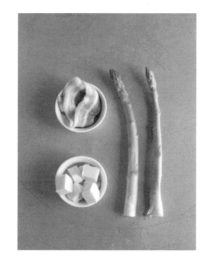

Figs

Roast a rack of pork for 1 hour at 160°C (315°F/Gas 2–3). Quarter 6 fresh figs and roughly chop 150 g (5½ oz) of dried figs. Arrange the figs around the roast 30 mins before the end of cooking, add 200 ml (7 fl oz) of port, then finish the cooking, basting the roast regularly with the cooking juices.

4 IDEAS

FOR SERVING
RACK OF PORK

Potatoes and chanterelle mushrooms

Dice 600 g (1 lb 5 oz) of new potatoes and sauté in the pork's roasting tin. Deglaze with a glass of white wine, then roast for 15 mins. Next, add 300 g (10½ oz) of chanterelle mushrooms (or other mushrooms) and cook for 10 mins. Add 300 ml (10½ fl oz) of crème fraîche and reduce until the sauce thickens.

Peaches

Roast a rack of pork for 1 hour at 160°C (315°F/Gas 2–3). Plunge 6 peaches into a saucepan of boiling water for a few seconds, remove the skin and slice into segments. Arrange the peaches around the roast 30 mins before the end of cooking time, then sprinkle with 50 g (1¾ oz) of brown sugar, a pinch of cinnamon, and deglaze with 200 ml (7 fl oz) of white port. Return to the oven for 30 mins, basting the roast with its cooking juices.

Rôti de cochon à la bière brune et aux pruneaux

ROAST PORK WITH
BROWN ALE AND PRUNES

1.25 kg (2 lb 12 oz) rolled pork loin
3 French shallots, peeled and diced
2 carrots, peeled and diced
1 teaspoon ground cinnamon
1 teaspoon ground ginger
60 ml (2 fl oz/¼ cup) olive oil
500 ml (17 fl oz/2 cups) brown ale
200 g (7 oz) pitted prunes
100 g (3½ oz) dried apricots
100 g (3½ oz) butter

Preheat the oven to 160°C
(315°F/Gas 2–3).

Combine the shallot, carrot,
cinnamon and ginger and mix well.

Heat the olive oil in a flameproof
roasting tin. Add the pork and brown
over high heat. Add the combined
vegetables and spices, then roast
in the oven for 30 minutes. Baste
the roast regularly with the ale.

Remove the roast and add the prunes
and dried apricots. Season with
salt and pepper, then return to the
oven for a further 30 minutes.

Transfer the roast to a serving plate.

To make the sauce, add the butter to the
roasting tin and stir well over low heat
into a sauce. Pour over the pork and serve.

Rôti de cochon au thé Earl Grey

ROAST PORK WITH
EARL GREY TEA

1.25 kg (2lb 12 oz) pork shoulder
60 ml (2 fl oz/¼ cup) olive oil
6 French shallots, peeled and
roughly chopped
6 garlic cloves, roughly chopped
2 Earl Grey teabags
6 potatoes, unpeeled and halved
4 lemongrass stems, split lengthways
50 g (1¾ oz) fresh ginger, peeled and sliced
50 g (1¾ oz) butter
1 small bunch coriander (cilantro)

Preheat the oven to 150°C (300°F/Gas 2).

Heat the olive oil in a flameproof roasting
tin. Add the pork and brown on all sides
over high heat until it caramelises. Add
the shallot and garlic and combine.

Infuse the teabags in 500 ml (7 fl oz/
2 cups) of boiling water.

Pour half the tea over the pork and roast
in the oven for 1 hour, basting regularly.

Remove the roast and arrange the
potato, lemongrass and ginger
around the meat. Pour the rest of
the tea over the roast, then return
to the oven for a further 1 hour.

Add the butter, scatter over coriander,
and season with salt and pepper. Then
allow the roast to rest in its juices,
covered in foil, for 10 minutes before
serving.

SERVES 6

PREPARATION TIME
20 minutes

COOKING TIME
1 hour

SERVES 6

PREPARATION TIME
15 minutes

COOKING TIME
2 hours

Rôti de cochon à la moutarde de Dijon
ROAST PORK WITH DIJON MUSTARD

1.25 kg (2 lb 12 oz) rolled pork loin
50 g (1¾ oz) butter
1 bunch bulb spring onions (scallions), sliced
3 leeks, halved
500 ml (17 fl oz/2 cups) white burgundy
3 turnips, peeled and halved
6 potatoes, peeled
300 ml (10½ fl oz) cream
2 tablespoons Dijon mustard
2 egg yolks
6 chives, snipped

Heat the butter in a flameproof casserole dish. Add the pork
and brown on all sides over medium heat. Add the spring
onion and the leek. Add half the wine and season with salt
and pepper. Reduce to a low heat, then cover and cook for
1 hour, making sure there is always some liquid in the dish.
Add the turnip, potatoes and the rest of the wine, and cook
for a further 20 minutes, covered.

Meanwhile, warm the cream over low heat.

Transfer the pork onto a serving dish and arrange the vegetables
around it.

Add the warm cream to the casserole dish and reduce the sauce
over low heat for 10 minutes, until it thickens. Remove from
the heat.

Put the sauce, mustard and egg yolks in a food processor and
blend until well combined. Pour the mustard sauce* over the roast
and garnish with the chives before serving.

*Note: The sauce can only be reheated over a very gentle heat,
not more than 85°C (185°F); otherwise it will curdle.

| SERVES 6 | PREPARATION TIME
15 minutes | COOKING TIME
1 hour 30 minutes |

Poitrine de cochon rôtie à la coriandre
ROAST PORK BELLY WITH CORIANDER

1.25 kg (2 lb 12 oz) pork belly
2 tablespoons ground coriander
2 tablespoons brown sugar
100 ml (3½ fl oz) olive oil, plus extra 2 tablespoons
6 carrots, peeled and diced
6 bulb spring onions (scallions), sliced
3 leeks, sliced
1 litre (35 fl oz/4 cups) white wine

The day before, remove the bones from the pork belly, taking care to remove all of them. Combine the coriander with the brown sugar, then add the olive oil. Rub the mixture generously all over the pork belly, wrap it tightly in plastic wrap and put in the refrigerator for 24 hours.

The next day, preheat the oven to 160°C (315°F/Gas 2–3).

Heat 2 tablespoons of olive oil in a flameproof roasting tin. Add the pork belly and brown on all sides over high heat. Add the carrot, onion and leek and allow to colour. Add the white wine, then roast in the oven for 2 hours. Turn the pork belly every 15 minutes during cooking, basting with the juices. If necessary, add water. For a crispy rind, increase the oven temperature to 200°C (400°F/Gas 6) in the final 15 minutes of cooking and turn the roast rind-side up.

Transfer the pork and vegetables onto a serving plate.

Reduce the cooking juices over low heat, then pour the juices over the stewed vegetables and sliced pork.

| SERVES 6 | PREPARATION - RESTING TIME 20 minutes - 24 hours | COOKING TIME 2 hours |

Échine confite au gingembre

SLOW-COOKED PORK
LOIN WITH GINGER

1.25 kg (2 lb 12 oz) pork loin
50 g (1¾ oz) butter
4 garlic cloves, finely chopped
1 teaspoon paprika
1 teaspoon sesame seeds
1 bunch sage, leaves only
100 g (3½ oz) fresh ginger, peeled and
sliced into 5 mm (¼ inch) sticks
50 g (1¾ oz) hazelnuts, roughly chopped
2 tablespoons olive oil

Preheat the oven to 150°C (300°F/Gas 2).

Heat the butter in a saucepan and
sauté the garlic over medium heat,
until it turns a lovely nutty brown.
Add the paprika and sesame seeds.

Slice the piece of pork crossways,
so that it opens like a book and
looks like a long rectangle.

Top the loin with the garlic butter
mixture, then scatter over the sage leaves,
ginger and hazelnut. Season with salt
and pepper. Reshape the roast by rolling
it up, then fasten it tightly with kitchen
string tied at 2 cm (¾ in) intervals.

Heat the olive oil in a flameproof
roasting tin. Add the pork loin and
brown over high heat. Put the pork
in the oven and roast for 2 hours,
basting it regularly with the cooking
juices. If necessary, add a little water.

Échine rôtie endives–oranges

ROAST PORK LOIN WITH
WITLOF AND ORANGE

1.25 kg (2 lb 12 oz) pork shoulder
zest and juice of 4 oranges
zest and juice of 1 lemon
200 ml (7 fl oz) white port
60 ml (2 fl oz/¼ cup) olive oil
6 witlof (chicory/Belgian endive),
halved lengthways
6 French shallots, peeled and thinly sliced
80 g (2¾ oz) butter

Preheat the oven to 150°C (300°F/Gas 2).

Combine the zest and juice of the oranges
and lemon with the port and mix well.

Heat the olive oil in a flameproof roasting
tin. Add the pork and brown over
medium heat until well caramelised.

Arrange the witlof and shallot around
the pork, pour over the port mixture
and season with salt and pepper. Dot
the top of the pork with small knobs of
butter, then roast in the oven for 1 hour
30 minutes, regularly basting the witlof
and the meat with the cooking juices.

SERVES 6
PREPARATION TIME
15 minutes
COOKING TIME
2 hours

SERVES 6
PREPARATION TIME
15 minutes
COOKING TIME
1 hour 30 minutes

Échine rôtie au bacon et au comté

ROAST PORK LOIN WITH BACON
AND COMTÉ CHEESE

1.25 kg (2 lb 12 oz) pork loin
4 tablespoons olive oil
6 sweet onions, peeled and sliced into rings
6 slices bacon
200 ml (7 fl oz) white port
200 g (7 oz) comté or gruyère cheese, sliced
6 chives, snipped

Preheat the oven to 180°C (350°F/Gas 4).

Heat 2 tablespoons of olive oil in a non-stick frying pan and
fry the onion over medium heat until lightly golden.

Grill the bacon under a griller until crisp.

Heat the remaining olive oil in a flameproof roasting tin. Add
the pork and brown on all sides over high heat. Add the port,
then roast in the oven for 1 hour 20 minutes, basting the
pork regularly with the cooking juices.

Remove the roast from the oven and allow the pork to rest
for 5 minutes in its juices, then make 6 cuts two-thirds of
the way through the roast. In each cut place some fried onion,
a slice of bacon and a slice of comté cheese. Season with salt
and pepper, then return to the oven for another 10 minutes.
Serve with chives.

| SERVES 6 | PREPARATION TIME
20 minutes | COOKING TIME
1 hour 40 minutes |

Travers rôti, ail grillé

ROAST SPARE RIBS WITH TOASTED GARLIC

1.25 kg (2 lb 12 oz) pork ribs
8 garlic cloves, chopped
2 French shallots, peeled and chopped
100 g (3½ oz) peanuts, chopped
1 bunch coriander (cilantro), finely chopped
80 g (2¾ oz) tomato sauce (ketchup)
150 ml (5 fl oz) soy sauce
100 ml (3½ fl oz) olive oil
3 onions, peeled and halved
2 leeks, halved
1 celery stalk, halved
1 bouquet garni

Preheat the oven to 180°C (350°F/Gas 4).

Combine the garlic, shallot, peanut and
coriander with the tomato sauce, soy sauce and
olive oil and mix well into a marinade.

Put the onion, leek and celery into a large pot of water
and allow to simmer over low heat. Add the bouquet
garni, then immerse the ribs and simmer for 30 minutes
over medium-low heat, skimming regularly.

Transfer the ribs to a flameproof roasting tin. Cover them
with the marinade so that they are well coated, then roast
the ribs in the oven for about 15 minutes, making sure the
meat is well basted with the marinade. The ribs should
have a glazed appearance and the meat should come away
from the bones.

| SERVES 6 | PREPARATION TIME
15 minutes | COOKING TIME
45 minutes |

20 minutes

10 minutes

30 minutes

Vendredi
POISSON EN RÔTI

Friday
is roast fish

Rôti de saumon aux herbes fraîches

ROAST SALMON WITH
FRESH HERBS

2 kg (4 lb 8 oz) salmon
3 tablespoons olive oil, plus extra
6 onions, peeled and sliced
200 ml (7 fl oz) white wine
30 g (1 oz) fresh ginger, peeled
1 French shallot, peeled
1 small bunch basil, leaves only
1 small bunch tarragon, leaves only
1 small bunch chervil, leaves only
2 Melba toasts
100 g (3½ oz) butter

Remove the salmon head. Cut away the two sides of salmon, retaining the skin. Trim the tail 5 cm (2 in) from the end. Use tweezers to remove the bones from the salmon fillets.

Preheat the oven to 160°C (315°F/Gas 2–3).

Heat the olive oil in a large non-stick frying pan. Add the onion and sauté over medium heat until soft. Deglaze with white wine and reduce for 5 minutes. Season with salt and pepper, then pour the mixture into a flameproof roasting tin.

Put the ginger, shallot, the basil, tarragon and chervil leaves, Melba toast and butter in a food processor. Blend ingredients until smooth, then season with salt and pepper.

Spread the herb mixture generously over 1 salmon fillet, skin-side down, then cover with the other and tie together with string.

Lay the salmon parcel on top of the softened onion, drizzle over a little olive oil, then bake in the oven for 10 minutes. Turn the salmon over and continue to cook for another 10 minutes.

Rôti de saumon fumé et cabillaud à la moutarde d'estragon

ROAST COD WITH
SMOKED SALMON AND
TARRAGON MUSTARD

1 kg (2 lb 4 oz) cod fillet
zest and juice of 1 orange
1 tablespoon coriander seeds, crushed
1 tablespoon tarragon mustard
4 large slices smoked salmon
olive oil
150 ml (5 fl oz) white wine
1 small bunch tarragon, leaves only
4 French shallots, peeled and chopped
150 ml (5 fl oz) fish stock
200 ml (7 fl oz) cream

The day before, slice the cod fillet open lengthways, then roll it into a sausage shape.

Combine well the orange zest and juice, coriander and tarragon mustard.

Spread the mixture over the rolled cod and wrap it tightly in plastic wrap to make an even shape. Put in the refrigerator for 24 hours.

The next day, place the roll in the freezer for 10 minutes, then remove the plastic wrap.

Preheat the oven to 100°C (200°F/Gas ½).

Wrap cod parcel in the smoked salmon slices and tie with string. Put the cod in a roasting tin and brush with olive oil. Pour over the white wine and bake in the oven for 45 minutes.

Chop the tarragon leaves. Put the tarragon, shallot and fish stock in a saucepan and combine well over medium heat and reduce by half. Add the cream and reduce again by half. Season with salt and pepper. Serve the cod dressed with the sauce.

SERVES 6
PREPARATION TIME
30 minutes
COOKING TIME
20 minutes

SERVES 6
PREPARATION TIME - MARINATING TIME
20 minutes - 24 hours
COOKING TIME
45 minutes

Rôti de saumon aux crevettes

ROAST SALMON WITH PRAWNS

1 side of salmon, skinned and pin-boned
2 French shallots, peeled and chopped
1 bunch parsley, chopped
100 ml (3½ fl oz) cream
1 teaspoon aniseed
1 egg
150 g (5½ oz) small prawns, shelled
50 ml (1¾ fl oz) pastis
50 g (1¾ oz) butter
2 garlic cloves, chopped
6 extra large Mediterranean prawns

Cut the fillet into three pieces. Put the two fleshier
pieces aside and dice the tail end into small cubes.

Preheat the oven to 180°C (350°F/Gas 4).

Put the diced salmon, shallot, half the parsley, cream,
aniseed and egg in a food processor. Blend ingredients
until smooth, then season with salt and pepper.

Combine the salmon mixture and the small prawns in a bowl.

Rub the middle of the remaining two pieces of salmon
with the pastis. Make 1 cm (½ in) cuts in the salmon
and spread with the salmon-prawn filling. Close
up like a book and tie together with string.

Heat the butter in a flameproof roasting tin. Add the garlic
and then the salmon parcel and brown on all sides over
medium heat. Bake in the oven for 7 minutes, then remove
and add the Mediterranean prawns and bake for a further
7 minutes. Scatter over the rest of the parsley before serving.

| SERVES 6 | PREPARATION TIME
30 minutes | COOKING TIME
15 minutes |

Rôti de lotte aux coques
ROAST MONKFISH WITH COCKLES

1 kg (2 lb 4 oz) monkfish
1 kg (2 lb 4 oz) cockles
1 teaspoon plain (all-purpose) flour
50 g (1 ¾ oz) butter
2 tablespoons olive oil, plus extra
5 garlic cloves, chopped
2 French shallots, peeled and chopped
1 bunch chives, finely chopped
100 ml (3½ fl oz) white wine
200 ml (7 fl oz) cream

Preheat the oven to 180°C (350°F/Gas 4).

Rinse the cockles well in a large quantity of
cold water to remove all the sand.

Combine the flour and butter together well in a bowl.

Remove the backbone, head and tail of the monkfish, join the
two fillets together head-to-tail and tie with string. Brush the
fillets with the extra olive oil and season with salt and pepper.

Bake the monkfish in a flameproof roasting tin in the oven
for 15 minutes. Transfer the monkfish to a serving dish,
but retain the cooking juices in the roasting tin.

Heat 2 tablespoons of olive oil in a non-stick frying pan. Add the
garlic, shallot and chives and sauté over medium heat. Deglaze
with the white wine. Pour the sauce into the roasting tin. Add the
cockles and simmer over low heat on the stovetop for 2 minutes,
just until the cockles open.

Strain the cooking juices through a sieve into a saucepan
and bring it to the boil. Add the floured butter and mix
well. Add the cream and reduce until the sauce thickens.

Pour the sauce over the monkfish and serve.

SERVES 6	PREPARATION TIME	COOKING TIME
	10 minutes	20 minutes

Rôti de lotte, poitrine fumée et olives noires
ROAST MONKFISH WITH SMOKY
BACON AND BLACK OLIVES

1.25 kg (2 lb 12 oz) monkfish
200 g (7 oz) dry-salted black olives, pitted
1 branch rosemary, leaves only
1 teaspoon ground cumin
12 thin slices smoked bacon
2 tablespoons olive oil, plus extra
1 kg (2 lb 4 oz) English spinach, stalks removed

The day before, preheat the oven to 100°C (200°F/Gas ½).

Arrange the olives on a baking tray lined with baking
paper and dry them out in the oven for 6 hours.

The next day, put the olives, rosemary leaves and cumin
in a food processor and blend until well combined.

Preheat the oven to 160°C (315°F/Gas 2–3).

Remove the backbone of the monkfish and separate the
two fillets. Spread the olive mixture down the middle
of the fillets and put them together head-to-tail.

Lay out the slices of bacon so that they overlap the whole
length of the monkfish, then roll it all up and tie with
string. Brush the monkfish roll with a little olive oil.

Heat 2 tablespoons of olive oil in a flameproof
roasting tin. Add the monkfish roll and brown over
low heat, then bake in the oven for 15 minutes.

Transfer the monkfish to a serving plate. Add a little
olive oil to the roasting tin and sauté the spinach. Season
with salt and pepper, and serve with the monkfish.

| SERVES 6 | PREPARATION TIME
20 minutes | COOKING TIME
20 minutes + 6 hours |

Bar rôti au fenouil
ROAST SEA BASS WITH FENNEL

2 kg (4 lb 8 oz) whole sea bass
1 tablespoon fennel seeds
2 fennel bulbs, finely sliced
zest and juice of 1 lemon
50 g (1¾ oz) butter
3 French shallots, peeled and chopped
3 fresh lemon thyme sprigs, leaves only
olive oil

Using a very sharp knife, remove the backbone of the bass, keeping the fillets attached, by following the backbone from tail to head on both sides. Cut the bone at the head and tail ends: the bass will then have its initial shape but without the backbone.

Preheat the oven to 180°C (350°F/Gas 4).

Sprinkle the fillets with fennel seeds.

Cook the fennel slices with the lemon juice in boiling salted water until tender. Drain.

Heat the butter in a non-stick frying pan. Add the shallot and fennel and soften them over low heat. Add the lemon zest and thyme and sauté over low heat for 2 minutes. Season with salt and pepper.

Stuff the fennel mixture inside the bass and tie it up. Place the bass on a baking tray lined with baking paper. Brush with olive oil and bake in the oven for 20 minutes.

Serve the bass with extra virgin olive oil and fine sea salt.

Dorade rôtie et anchoyade
ROASTED SEA BREAM WITH ANCHOIADE

12 sea bream fillets, skin on and
   pin-boned
2 garlic cloves
150 g (5½ oz) dry-salted black
   olives, pitted
4 anchovies in oil
100 ml (3½ fl oz) olive oil, plus
   extra to drizzle
2 yellow capsicums (peppers)
150 g (5½ oz) sun-dried tomatoes
in oil, finely sliced

Preheat the oven to 190°C (375°F/Gas 5).

Put the garlic, black olives, anchovies and olive oil in a food processor. Blend the combined ingredients until smooth.

Cut the capsicums into large flat pieces and remove the seeds and membrane. Cook skin-side up in the oven for 10 minutes, or until the skin blackens and blisters. Remove from the oven and seal in a plastic bag for 10 minutes, until cool. Remove the skin and finely slice.

Put the capsicum, sun-dried tomato and olive-anchovy mixture into a bowl and combine well.

Increase the oven temperature to 200°C (400°F/Gas 6).

Lay 6 fillets skin-side down on a tray lined with baking paper, and spread the capsicum-anchoiade mixture over them. Cover with the other fillets skin-side up and drizzle over a little olive oil. Bake in the oven for 8 minutes, then serve immediately.

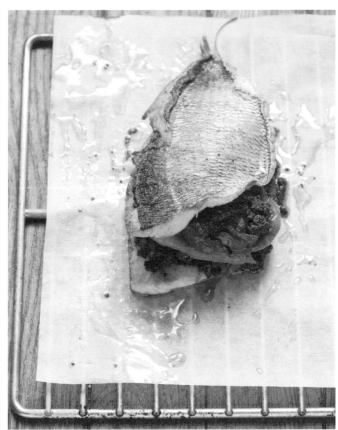

SERVES 6
PREPARATION TIME
30 minutes
COOKING TIME
25 minutes

SERVES 6
PREPARATION TIME
20 minutes
COOKING TIME
20 minutes

Rôti de cabillaud à la sauge

ROAST COD WITH SAGE

1.25 kg (2 lb 12 oz) cod fillet
50 ml (1¾ fl oz) olive oil, plus extra 2 tablespoons
500 g (1 lb 2 oz) chanterelle mushrooms
3 French shallots, peeled and finely sliced
3 swedes (rutabaga), peeled and cut into wedges
6 bulb spring onions (scallions), halved
12 sage leaves
100 g (3½ oz) butter, diced
100 ml (3½ fl oz) white wine

Preheat the oven to 160°C (315°F/Gas 2–3).

Heat 2 tablespoons of extra olive oil in a non-stick frying pan. Add the mushrooms and shallot and sauté them over medium heat until all their water has been released. Set aside in a bowl.

Cook the swede for 15 minutes in boiling salted water.

Heat the olive oil in the frying pan. Add the cod fillet and brown on all sides over medium heat.

Arrange the mushroom mixture, swede and spring onion in a flameproof casserole dish. Scatter over the sage leaves and butter, then pour over the white wine. Lay the cod fillet on top, season with fine sea salt, then bake in the oven for 15 minutes.

| SERVES 6 | PREPARATION TIME
20 minutes | COOKING TIME
30 minutes |

Thon rôti serrano–basilic

ROASTED TUNA WITH SERRANO HAM AND BASIL

1 kg (2 lb 4 oz) tuna fillet
1 garlic clove, finely chopped
10 g (¼ oz) fresh ginger
200 ml (7 fl oz) olive oil
1 bunch basil, leaves only
6 slices Serrano ham

Preheat the oven to 180°C (350°F/Gas 4).

Combine the garlic, ginger and 100 ml (3½ fl oz) of the
olive oil in a bowl and mix well.

Make a cut down the middle of the tuna fillet and brush inside
with the garlic-oil mixture. Season with salt and pepper,
then insert basil leaves along the length of the fillet.

Roll the tuna in the garlic-oil mixture, wrap in
slices of cured ham, then tie with string.

Heat the remaining olive oil in a flameproof roasting tin.
Add the tuna parcel and brown over medium heat, then bake
in the oven for 10 minutes. Be careful not to overcook, as tuna
should be eaten very red.

Sprinkle with fine sea salt just before serving.

| SERVES 6 | PREPARATION TIME
20 minutes | COOKING TIME
10 minutes |

Rôti de thon au sésame

ROAST TUNA WITH SESAME

1 kg (2 lb 4 oz) tuna fillet
100 ml (3½ fl oz) soy sauce
100 ml (3½ fl oz) fish sauce
1 teaspoon ground cardamom
1 teaspoon aniseed
5 tablespoons olive oil
1 tablespoon sesame seeds
2 carrots, peeled and finely sliced
1 fennel bulb, finely sliced
1 cucumber, seeded and finely sliced

Combine the soy sauce, fish sauce, cardamom, aniseed and
1 tablespoon of olive oil in a large shallow dish and mix well.
Marinate the tuna in the mixture, covered, for 1 hour in
the refrigerator.

Roll the tuna in the sesame seeds.

Heat 2 tablespoons of olive oil in a non-stick frying pan.
Add the tuna parcel and brown it on all sides over medium heat.
Make sure that the tuna is not overcooked: the tuna should be
eaten very rare; however bake it further in the oven if you'd
prefer it more cooked.

Heat the remaining olive oil in a wok. Add the carrot, fennel
and cucumber and sauté them with 2 tablespoons of the
marinade, then serve immediately with the tuna.

Dill

Remove the backbone via the back of the fish while keeping the two fillets attached to the body: slide a knife along the backbone, then cut the bone at the head and tail end. Finely chop 1 bunch of dill. Zest 1 lime and combine it with the dill. Sprinkle the flesh with chilli powder and cover with the dill mixture. Tie the fish up with string, drizzle over a little olive oil, then bake in the oven.

Fresh herbs

Put together 1 bunch of basil, 3 celery stalks, 1 bunch of chives, 1 French shallot, 1 bunch of tarragon, 1 lemon thyme sprig, 100 g (3½ oz) of butter and 100 g (3½ oz) of dry bread into a food processor. Blend all of the ingredients into a smooth paste. Season with salt and pepper. Remove the backbone of the fish via the back without detaching the two fillets. Fill the fish with the herb paste, then bake in the oven.

4 IDEAS

FOR STUFFING
FISH

Fish stuffing

Put 200 g (7 oz) of white-fleshed fish, 100 ml (3½ fl oz) of cream, 1 egg and 1 bunch of snipped chives into a food processor and blend into a smooth mixture. Season with salt and pepper. Remove the backbone of the fish via the back without detaching the two fillets. Stuff the fish with the mixture, tie the two fillets together with string, then bake in the oven.

Aniseed

Remove the backbone of the fish via the back without detaching the two fillets. Slice 2 garlic cloves. Brush the flesh of the fish with pastis and lay the slices of garlic all along its length. Season with freshly ground black pepper, drizzle over a little olive oil, then bake in the oven.

Samedi

ÇA RÔTIT POUR DE

L'AGNEAU

Saturday
is roast lamb

Gigot tout simplement
ROAST LEG OF LAMB,
PLAIN AND SIMPLE

1 leg of lamb
1 bulb garlic
1 thyme sprig
1 rosemary sprig
80 ml (2½ fl oz/⅓ cup) olive oil,
plus extra 2 tablespoons

Prepare the lamb leg using one of
the following three methods:

1 – The day before, stud the leg with
the garlic cloves and rub the leg with
olive oil. Break the thyme and rosemary
into smaller pieces and scatter over
the leg. Wrap the lamb in plastic
wrap and keep in the refrigerator.

2 – Finely chop 3 garlic cloves. Combine
the garlic, chopped thyme and rosemary
and olive oil in a container with a lid and
mix well. Allow the mixture to infuse for
24 hours in the refrigerator. The next day,
rub the flavoured oil all over the lamb.

3 – Finely chop all the garlic, thyme and
rosemary, and combine well with the
olive oil. Make small cuts in the lamb
leg and rub the herb mixture all over
the leg so that the earthy flavours of the
garrigue penetrate well into the meat.

Preheat the oven to 200°C (400°F/Gas 6).

Heat 2 tablespoons of olive oil in a
flameproof roasting tin. Add the lamb
and brown over high heat until it is well
caramelised. Transfer to the oven and
roast for 1 hour, basting regularly. Allow
the lamb to rest in its juices, covered
with foil, for 10 minutes before serving.

Note: Allow about 20 minutes per
kilogram for a leg that's pink in the
middle, but the shape of the leg (more or
less plump at the thick end) can affect the
cooking time. Test by inserting a skewer
into the middle of the leg; if it comes out
lukewarm to the touch, the leg is ready.

Gigot de 7 heures
7-HOUR ROAST LAMB

1 leg of lamb
2 tablespoons olive oil
5 French shallots, peeled
15 garlic cloves
and cut into wedges
2 branches rosemary
2 branches thyme
500 ml (7 fl oz) white wine
3 swedes (rutabaga), peeled

Preheat the oven to 120°C
(235°F/Gas ½).

Heat the olive oil in a flameproof
roasting tin. Add the leg of lamb and
brown on all sides over high heat.

Arrange the shallots, garlic, rosemary
and thyme around the lamb. Pour
over the white wine, then roast in the
oven for 5 hours, basting the leg
regularly with the cooking juices.
If necessary, add a little water.

After 5 hours, remove the roast
and add the swede, then return
to the oven for another 2 hours.
Season with salt and pepper.

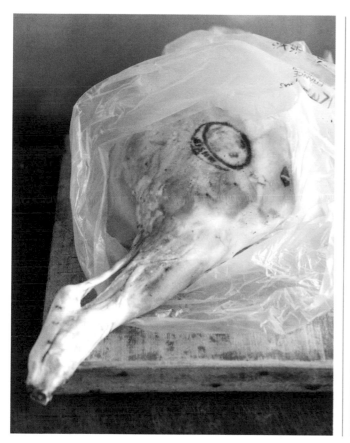

SERVES 6

PREPARATION - RESTING TIME
20 minutes - 24 hours

COOKING TIME
1 hour

SERVES 6

PREPARATION TIME
10 minutes

COOKING TIME
7 hours

Carrés d'agneau rôtis aux pistaches
ROAST RACKS OF LAMB WITH PISTACHIOS

2 racks of lamb with 6 ribs each
2 garlic cloves, chopped
2 French shallots, peeled and chopped
1 bunch basil, leaves only
1 bunch chervil, leaves only
80 g (2¾ oz) butter, chopped
4 slices sandwich bread
1 egg white
50 g (1¾ oz) pistachio kernels
olive oil

Preheat the oven to 200°C (400°F/Gas 6).

Put the garlic and shallot in a bowl, cover with boiling water
and set aside to soften. Drain.

Put the basil, chervil and butter in food processor and blend until
well combined. Add the bread and garlic and shallot mixture and
combine well. Add the egg white, season with salt and pepper
and blend until the mixture is smooth and well combined.

Add the pistachios to the herb butter and mix together. Spread the
mixture on the meat side of the racks, making sure it sticks onto
the meat.

Place the racks (herb-side up) in a roasting tin and drizzle over
a little olive oil. Roast in the oven for about 10 minutes. Allow
the racks to rest in their juices, covered with foil, for 5 minutes
before serving.

| SERVES 6 | PREPARATION TIME
20 minutes | COOKING TIME
15 minutes |

Carrés d'agneau en croûte de tomates confites

ROAST RACKS OF LAMB WITH A SUN-DRIED TOMATO CRUST

2 racks of lamb with 6 ribs each
6 witlof (chicory/Belgian
endive), halved lengthways
juice of 4 oranges and
zest of 2 oranges
200 ml (7 fl oz) white wine
100 ml (3½ fl oz) white port
50 g (1¾ oz) butter
300 g (10½ oz) sun-dried tomatoes in oil
6 French shallots, peeled
and finely chopped
2 tablespoons olive oil
1 egg white, beaten
1 bunch parsley, chopped

Preheat the oven to 160°C
(315°F/Gas 2–3).

Arrange the witlof in a flameproof
roasting tin. Pour over the orange juice,
wine and port and top with the butter.
Season with salt and pepper, then bake
in the oven for 30 minutes, turning
the witlof regularly.

Roughly process the sun-dried
tomatoes with the orange zest in a
food processor, then add the shallot
and mix together. Set aside.

Heat the olive oil in a non-stick
frying pan. Add the racks of lamb
and colour them over high heat.

Brush the back of the rack with egg white,
spread the sun-dried tomato mixture
on top and season with salt and pepper.
Lay the racks on the witlof, then roast
for 15 minutes in the oven. Scatter with
chopped parsley just before serving.

Carrés d'agneau rôtis au miel et à la menthe

ROAST RACKS OF LAMB WITH HONEY AND MINT

2 racks of lamb with 6 ribs each
2 bunches mint, chopped
3 garlic cloves, chopped
4 tablespoons honey
6 potatoes, peeled and chopped into chunks
300 ml (10½ fl oz) cream
2 tablespoons olive oil

The day before, combine mint and garlic
and mix with 1 tablespoon of honey.
Spread the racks generously with the
honey mint, wrap them in plastic wrap
and put in the refrigerator for 24 hours.

The next day, cook the potato in a
large pot of boiling salted water for
30 minutes. Add the cream to the potato
and pureé with a handheld blender. Add
the remaining honey, season with salt
and pepper and combine well.

Preheat the oven to 180°C (350°F/Gas 4).

Heat the olive oil in a flameproof roasting
tin. Add the racks of lamb and brown
on all sides over high heat. Transfer
to the oven and roast for 10 minutes.
Season with salt and pepper. Allow the
lamb to rest in its juices, covered with
foil, for 5 minutes before serving.

SERVES 6

PREPARATION TIME
30 minutes

COOKING TIME
45 minutes

SERVES 6

PREPARATION TIME -
RESTING TIME
20 minutes - 24 hours

COOKING TIME
40 minutes

Filet d'agneau rôti au pesto
ROAST LAMB LOIN WITH PESTO

2 racks of lamb with 6 ribs each*
1 bunch basil, leaves only, plus extra
100 g (3½ oz) parmesan cheese, diced,
    plus extra shavings to serve
50 g (1¾ oz) pine nuts, toasted
1 garlic clove
100 ml (3½ fl oz) olive oil, plus extra 2 tablespoons
600 g (1 lb 5 oz) cherry truss tomatoes

Preheat the oven to 200°C (400°F/Gas 6).

Put the basil, diced parmesan, pine nuts, garlic and olive
oil in a food processor. Blend until the ingredients form
a smooth pesto paste. Season with salt and pepper.

Put the lamb fillets in a flameproof roasting tin and brush
with 2 tablespoons of olive oil. Use the pointed end of a knife
and make an incision along the length of each fillet, and
spread generously with the pesto. Arrange the cherry tomatoes
around the fillets, then roast in the oven for 8 minutes.

Allow the fillets to rest in their juices, covered with
foil, for 5 minutes, then scatter with basil and shavings
of parmesan. Season with salt and pepper.

*Ask your butcher to bone the racks of lamb so that you only
have the fillet.

| SERVES 6 | PREPARATION TIME
10 minutes | COOKING TIME
10 minutes |

Sausage meat

Peel and chop 3 French shallots. Finely chop 1 bunch of chives. Combine well the shallot and chives with 200 g (7 oz) of sausage meat. Add 150 ml (5 fl oz) of cream, 50 g (1¾ oz) whole hazelnuts and 50 g (1¾ oz) of blanched almonds and mix well. Season with salt and pepper. Stuff the mixture into the lamb shoulder and tie with string.

Zucchini

Chop 3 garlic cloves and zest and juice 1 orange. Seed and dice 2 zucchini (courgettes). Heat 3 tablespoons of olive oil in a non-stick frying pan and sauté the zucchini over medium heat. Add the garlic, orange zest and juice. Scatter with a few lemon thyme sprigs, then allow the liquid to evaporate over low heat. Season with salt and pepper. Stuff the mixture into the lamb shoulder and tie well with string.

4 IDEAS

FOR STUFFING
LAMB SHOULDER

Fresh herbs

Make up a bouquet of wild fennel, lemon thyme, rosemary, sage and basil. Season the lamb shoulder with salt and pepper. Lay the herb bouquet in the middle of the shoulder, roll up and tie with string.

Pesto

Process 1 bunch of basil, 3 garlic cloves, 50 g (1¾ oz) of parmesan cheese, 50 g (1¾ oz) of pine nuts and 3 tablespoons of olive oil in a food processor until the ingredients form a smooth pesto paste. Stuff the lamb shoulder with the pesto and tie with string.

Épaule d'agneau rôtie au cumin
ROAST LAMB SHOULDER WITH CUMIN

1 lamb shoulder
2 tablespoons olive oil
3 French shallots, peeled
3 garlic cloves
1 tablespoon cumin seeds
200 ml (7 fl oz) white wine
½ cauliflower, cut into small florets
3 carrots, peeled and julienned
3 zucchini (courgettes), julienned
1 cucumber, peeled and julienned
50 g (1¾ oz) butter

Preheat the oven to 200°C (400°F/Gas 6).

Rub the lamb shoulder with the oil and season with salt
and pepper. Put the lamb in a flameproof roasting tin
and brown over high heat. Add the shallots, garlic and
cumin, then roast in the oven for 40 minutes.

Remove the roast and pour over the white wine. Add
the cauliflower, carrot, zucchini and cucumber and
return to the oven for a further 15 minutes.

Add the butter and mix it well with the
vegetables and serve immediately.

Épaule en cocotte de foin
LAMB SHOULDER IN A BED OF STRAW

1 boned lamb shoulder
200 g (7 oz) plain (all-purpose) flour
2 tablespoons olive oil
3 garlic cloves
3 French shallots
2–3 rosemary sprigs
3 bay leaves
300 ml (10½ fl oz) cider
100 g (3½ oz) butter
chemical-free straw

Preheat the oven to 160°C (315°F/Gas 2–3).

Combine the flour with some water to make
a smooth and pliable dough.

Heat the olive oil in a flameproof casserole dish. Add the
lamb shoulder and brown on all sides over high heat until it
is well caramelised. Add the garlic cloves, shallots, rosemary
and bay leaves. Deglaze with the cider. Add the butter and
mix in with the vegetables. Season with salt and pepper.

Surround the lamb with straw. Cover the dish and seal it with the
dough so that it is airtight. Bake in the oven for 1 hour 30 minutes.

Remove the roast from the oven and transfer the lamb to a serving
plate. Strain the cooking juices through a sieve and pour over
the shoulder.

SERVES 6	PREPARATION TIME	COOKING TIME
	10 minutes	1 hour 30 minutes

Souris d'agneau aux haricots tarbais
LAMB SHANKS WITH CANNELLINI BEANS

6 lamb hind shanks
50 g (1¾ oz) butter
4 garlic cloves
3 onions, peeled
8 anchovies in oil, finely chopped
300 g (10½ oz) dried cannellini beans
300 ml (10½ fl oz) white wine
700 ml (24 fl oz) lamb or veal stock
2 bay leaves
1 thyme sprig
400 g (14 oz) cherry tomatoes
100 g (3½ oz) cashews

Preheat the oven to 160°C (315°F/Gas 2–3).

Heat the butter in a flameproof casserole dish. Add the shanks and brown on all sides over high heat until they are well caramelised.

Add the garlic cloves and onions and brown them with the shanks. Then add the anchovy. Arrange the cannellini beans around the lamb. Pour over the white wine, then reduce over low heat for 15 minutes.

Add the lamb stock, bay leaves and thyme, and bake in the oven for 2 hours. Check the level of the cooking juices regularly to ensure that the beans are always sitting in liquid.

Remove from the oven and add the cherry tomatoes and cashews, then return to roast for a further 1 hour, until the beans are soft.

| SERVES 6 | PREPARATION TIME
20 minutes | COOKING TIME
3 hours |

10
minutes

Sweet and sour roasted fillet
of venison, page 136

20
minutes

Roast fillet of venison with sultanas, page 132
Roast leg of venison with pepper sauce, page 134
Fillet of wild boar with bilberries, page 138
Roast wild boar with black pepper, page 140

Dimanche MIDI
TROP DE LA CHANCE
C'EST RÔTI DE
GIBIER

Sunday lunch
is roast game

Filet de chevreuil aux raisins blonds

ROAST FILLET OF VENISON WITH SULTANAS

1.25 kg (2 lb 12 oz) venison fillet
100 g (3½ oz) sultanas
100 ml (3½ fl oz) armagnac
130 g (5 oz) butter
4 onions, peeled and cut into wedges
150 g (5½ oz) dried apricots
50 g (1¾ oz) fresh ginger, peeled and chopped
pinch of ground cinnamon
200 ml (7 fl oz) Sauternes

Plump up the sultanas in a large bowl of hot water
together with 1 tablespoon of the armagnac.

Heat 50 g (1¾ oz) of butter in a flameproof casserole
dish. Add the venison fillet and brown on all sides over
high heat until caramelised. Add the onion, deglaze
with the remaining armagnac, then flambé.

Arrange the dried apricots, drained sultanas and
ginger around the meat. Sprinkle with cinnamon,
cover, and cook over low heat for 5 minutes.

Add the Sauternes, then cook, uncovered, for 5 more minutes.
Add the remaining butter and cook for a further 5 minutes.

Transfer the venison to a carving board and allow it to rest,
covered with foil, for 5 minutes.

| SERVES 6 | PREPARATION TIME
20 minutes | COOKING TIME
20 minutes |

Cuisse de chevreuil rôtie, sauce poivrade
ROAST LEG OF VENISON WITH PEPPER SAUCE

2 kg (4 lb 8 oz) leg of venison, plus
    500 g (1 lb 2 oz) venison trimmings
150 g (5½ oz) pork fat, finely diced
3 onions, peeled and diced
3 carrots, peeled and diced
300 ml (10½ fl oz) good red wine
2 bay leaves
50 ml (1¾ fl oz) wine vinegar
1 teaspoon cracked black pepper
100 g (3½ oz) butter

1 bouquet garni
1 celeriac bulb, peeled and diced
300 ml (10½ fl oz) cream
1 tablespoon plain (all-purpose) flour

The day before, make small cuts all over the leg and insert
the pieces of pork fat.

To make the marinade, combine the onion, carrot, red wine,
bay leaves, vinegar and cracked pepper in a bowl and mix well.
Marinate the venison for 24 hours in the refrigerator, turning the
leg over regularly, so that the marinade is distributed evenly.

The next day, preheat the oven to 220°C (425°F/Gas 7).

Melt half the butter. Remove the venison from the marinade.
Place the venison in a flameproof roasting tin. Pour over
the melted butter and brown in the oven for 10 minutes.

Reduce the oven temperature to 180°C (350°F/ Gas 4).
Arrange the venison trimmings, garni and vegetables from
the marinade all around the joint. Return to the oven and
roast for 10 minutes per 500 g (1 lb 2 oz) for pink venison,
basting the meat regularly with its cooking juices.

Meanwhile, cook the celeriac in a saucepan of boiling salted water
for 30 minutes. Strain the water, then add the cream to the celeriac
and purée with a handheld blender. Season with salt and pepper.

Transfer the leg to a carving board. Put the roasting tin on the
stovetop, deglaze with the marinade and reduce over medium
heat. Strain the sauce and vegetables through a sieve into a
saucepan, pressing the vegetables well to extract the juice.

Combine well the flour and remaining butter, then add
to the saucepan with the juices. Whisk together until
the sauce thickens. Season with salt and pepper.

Pour the sauce over venison slices and serve with the
celeriac purée.

SERVES 6

PREPARATION TIME - 20 minutes
MARINATING TIME - 24 hours

COOKING TIME
40 minutes

Filet de biche rôti aigre-doux
SWEET AND SOUR ROASTED FILLET OF VENISON

1.25 kg (2 lb 12 oz) fillet of venison (doe)
100 g (3½ oz) butter
6 French shallots, peeled and chopped in half
150 ml (5 fl oz) white wine
50 ml (1¾ fl oz) gin
3 cooked beetroots (beets)*, halved
100 ml (3½ fl oz) balsamic vinegar
50 ml (1¾ fl oz) raspberry liqueur
1 small bunch chervil, roughly chopped

Preheat the oven to 200°C (400°F/Gas 6).

Heat 50 g (1¾ oz) of the butter in a flameproof roasting
tin. Add the venison and brown on all sides over high heat.
Add the shallot, then roast in the oven for 10 minutes.

Transfer the roast to a serving plate and allow it
to rest, covered with foil, for 10 minutes.

Put the roasting tin on the stovetop and deglaze with the
white wine and gin over medium heat, scraping any bits
stuck to the bottom of the tin well using a spatula. Add the
beetroot, balsamic vinegar and raspberry liqueur. Season
with salt and pepper. Reduce the sauce until it thickens.
Add the remaining butter and stir until well combined.

Dress the venison slices with the sauce and scatter over
chopped chervil.

*To cook the beetroot, bring a saucepan of salted water to the boil.
Add the beetroot bulbs and gently boil for 30–45 minutes, or until
tender when pierced with a skewer.

| SERVES 6 | PREPARATION TIME
10 minutes | COOKING TIME
20 minutes |

Filet de sanglier aux airelles

FILLET OF WILD BOAR WITH BILBERRIES

1.25 kg (2 lb 12 oz) fillet of wild boar
80 g (2¾ oz) butter
3 French shallots, peeled and finely sliced
50 ml (1¾ fl oz) balsamic vinegar
1 glass ruby or tawny port
50 ml (1¾ fl oz) crème de cassis
200 g (7 oz) bilberries

Heat 50 g (1¾ oz) of the butter in a flameproof casserole dish.
Add the meat and brown it over high heat, then reduce to
medium heat and let it caramelise on all sides for 5 minutes.

Arrange the shallot around the fillet, and continue to cook
for 2–3 minutes. Deglaze with balsamic vinegar and reduce for
10 minutes, or until the vinegar has completely evaporated.

Moisten with the port and the crème de cassis, add the
bilberries and cook for 5 minutes, covered, then add
the remaining butter. Season with salt and pepper.

| SERVES 6 | PREPARATION TIME
20 minutes | COOKING TIME
25 minutes |

Rôti de sanglier au poivre noir

ROAST WILD BOAR WITH BLACK PEPPER

1.25 kg (2 lb 12 oz) wild boar roast
50 g (1¾ oz) butter, melted
1 teaspoon crushed black pepper
5 French shallots, peeled and sliced
50 ml (1¾ fl oz) cognac
200 ml (7 fl oz) veal stock
300 ml (10½ fl oz) cream
600 g (1 lb 5 oz) chestnuts, roasted and peeled

Preheat the oven to 180°C (350°F/Gas 4).

Brush the meat with the butter, then roll it in the
crushed pepper.

Put the meat in a flameproof roasting tin. Arrange the
shallot around it and roast in the oven for 30 minutes,
basting the roast regularly.

Turn off the oven. Transfer the roast to a baking tray
and allow it to rest near an opened heated oven.

Put the roasting tin on the stovetop and deglaze with the
cognac, flambé them over medium heat. Then add the stock
and reduce by half.

Warm the cream in a saucepan, then add it to the sauce.
Season with salt and pepper.

Add the chestnuts to the roasting tin and heat gently in the
cream sauce. Return the roast to the tin and cover with the
sauce before serving.

| SERVES 6 | PREPARATION TIME
20 minutes | COOKING TIME
40 minutes |

The little bonuses

Dimanche SOIR
IL EN RESTE

Sunday evening
is all the rest

Boulettes à la tomate
MEATBALLS WITH TOMATO

Preheat the oven to 180°C (350°F/Gas 4).

Peel 3 French shallots and chop them very finely. Peel and chop 1 bunch of tarragon. Dice 4 tomatoes.

Brown 50 g (1¾ oz) of pine nuts in a non-stick frying pan.

Soak 2 slices of bread in 150 ml (5 fl oz) cream.

Chop 500 g (1 lb 2 oz) of leftover roast meat with the *pain d'épices*. Add the pine nuts, the shallot, tarragon and 3 eggs. Combine together well in a large bowl and season with salt and pepper.

Roll mixture into small meatballs and arrange in a flameproof casserole dish. Scatter over the diced tomato, drizzle over a little olive oil, then moisten with 100 ml (3½ fl oz) of white wine. Bake in the oven for 45 minutes.

Beignets de bœuf façon thaïe
THAI-STYLE BEEF CROQUETTES

Chop 6 garlic cloves. Slice 2 bulb spring onions (scallions). Zest 1 lemon and chop finely. Strip the leaves from 1 bunch of coriander (cilantro) and chop. Seed and slice 1 bird's eye chilli. Peel and chop 50 g (1¾ oz) of fresh ginger.

Combine all of the ingredients with 500 g (1 lb 2 oz) of leftover roast beef in a large bowl. Add 2 tablespoons of soy sauce and 1 tablespoon of fish sauce. Season with salt and pepper.

Beat 3 eggs and combine with 100 ml (3½ fl oz) cream.

Make small balls in the palm of your hand, then put them in a plastic bag and leave in the freezer for 10 minutes.

Dip the cold meatballs in the egg-cream mixture, then roll in 150 g (5½ oz) of powdered coconut. Repeat this process once.

Heat 100 ml (3½ fl oz) of olive oil on medium-high heat. Add the meatballs and cook until golden brown. Transfer onto kitchen paper to strain excess oil. Serve with a sweet and sour sauce.

Tomates farcies
STUFFED TOMATOES

Preheat the oven to 180°C (350°F/Gas 4).

Chop 3 garlic cloves. Peel and chop 3 French shallots. Heat 100 ml (3½ fl oz) of olive oil in a frying pan and sauté the garlic and shallot.

Chop 1 bunch of parsley. Soak 3 slices of sandwich bread in 150 ml (5 fl oz) of cream.

Chop 500 g (1 lb 2 oz) of leftover roast meat with 2 slices of ham and put in a bowl. Add the soaked bread, shallot, garlic and parsley and combine well. Season with salt and pepper.

Slice the tops off 6 large tomatoes and scoop out the flesh. Fill the tomatoes with the stuffing and replace the tomato tops.

Put the tomatoes in a roasting tin and arrange the scooped-out tomato flesh around the tomatoes. Drizzle generously with olive oil, then bake in the oven for 30 minutes.

Poivrons farcis
STUFFED CAPSICUMS

Preheat the oven to 180°C (350°F/Gas 4).

Peel and finely chop 4 onions. Slice the tops off 6 capsicums (peppers) of different colours and remove the seeds. Strip the leaves from 1 bunch of mint and finely chop. Chop 1 bunch of chives.

Chop up 500 g (1 lb 2 oz) of leftover roast pork.

Combine the meat and the chopped herbs and onion in a large bowl. Add 150 g (5½ oz) goat's cheese, 1 tablespoon of cumin seeds and 1 tablespoon of paprika. Season with salt and pepper.

Fill each capsicum with the stuffing and replace the capsicum tops.

Arrange the capsicums in a roasting tin and drizzle generously with olive oil. Bake in the oven for 30 minutes, basting regularly with 300 ml (10½ fl oz) of white wine throughout the cooking.

Lasagnes
LASAGNE

Preheat the oven to 180°C (350°F/Gas 4).

Peel and slice 4 onions. Dice 6 tomatoes. Strip the leaves from 1 bunch of basil and chop 500 g (1 lb 2 oz) of leftover roast meat.

Heat 100 ml (3½ fl oz) of olive oil in a large heavy-based saucepan. Sauté all of the ingredients over medium heat and allow the tomatoes to stew. Then add 2 tablespoons of tomato sauce (ketchup). Season with salt and pepper.

To make the béchamel sauce, melt 50 g (1¾ oz) butter in a saucepan. Add 50 g (1¾ oz) of plain (all-purpose) flour and cook for 3 minutes. Add 1 litre (35 fl oz/4 cups) of milk and allow the sauce to thicken.

Make a layer of béchamel sauce in a flameproof casserole dish. Scatter over some grated gruyère cheese and a layer of chopped meat, then cover with sheets of oven-ready lasagne. Make a series of layers until the ingredients are all used up, finishing with the béchamel sauce and grated cheese on top.

Bake in the oven for 45 minutes.

Cannellonis
CANNELLONI

Preheat the oven to 160°C (315°F/Gas 2–3).

Chop 500 g (1 lb 2 oz) of leftover roast meat. Peel and finely chop 3 onions. Finely chop 6 garlic cloves. Heat 100 ml (3½ fl oz) of olive oil in a frying pan and brown the onion and garlic over medium heat. Add the meat and 150 g (5½ oz) of thin strips of streaky bacon to the pan and sauté together. Add 1 teaspoon of ground cumin and 200 ml (7 fl oz) of cream and mix well. Season with salt and pepper. Fill 18 cannelloni with the stuffing.

To make the béchamel sauce, melt 50 g (1¾ oz) of butter in a saucepan. Add 50 g (1¾ oz) plain (all-purpose) flour and cook for 3 minutes. Add 1 litre (35 fl oz/4 cups) of milk and allow the sauce to thicken.

Heat 100 ml (3½ fl oz) of olive oil in another frying pan and sauté 600 g (1 lb 5 oz) of spinach. Add to the béchamel sauce and combine well. Season with salt and pepper.

Arrange the cannelloni in a flameproof casserole dish, cover with the spinach-béchamel sauce, then bake in the oven for 45 minutes.

Hachis parmentier
FRENCH SHEPHERD'S PIE

Preheat the oven to 160°C (315°F/Gas 2–3).

Peel 1 kg (2 lb 7 oz) of potatoes and chop into chunks. Cook them in boiling salted water for 30 minutes. Strain the excess water from the potatoes. Add 150 g (5½ oz) of butter and 1 teaspoon of nutmeg to the saucepan and purée with a handheld blender. Season with salt and pepper.

Chop 500 g (1 lb 2 oz) of leftover roast meat.

Peel and chop 4 onions, then sauté in 100 g (3½ oz) of duck fat over medium heat. Add the meat and 100 g (3½ oz) of roughly chopped hazelnuts. Season with salt and pepper.

Make a layer of meat in the base of a flameproof casserole dish. Cover with the potato mash and sprinkle with crushed melba toast. Bake in the oven for 30 minutes.

Moussaka
MOUSSAKA

Preheat the oven to 160°C (315°F/Gas 2–3).

Cut 3 eggplant (aubergines) into rounds. Season with salt and pepper and set aside for 1 hour. Slice 4 garlic cloves and peel and slice 3 onions. Strip the leaves from 1 bunch of mint and finely chop.

Chop 500 g (1 lb 2 oz) of leftover lamb. Heat 100 ml (3½ fl oz) of olive oil in a heavy-based frying pan. Add the meat, garlic, onion and mint and sauté over medium heat. Season.

Pan-fry the eggplant in olive oil, then drain on kitchen paper.

To make the sauce, melt 60 g (2¼ oz) of butter in a saucepan over medium heat. Add 60 g (2¼ oz) of plain (all-purpose) flour and cook for 5 minutes, then add 750 ml (26 fl oz/3 cups) of milk and allow the sauce to thicken. Then add 150 g (5½ oz) of grated gruyère cheese and season with salt and pepper.

Make a layer of eggplant slices in the base of a flameproof casserole dish. Cover with the meat, top with another layer of eggplant, cover with sauce, then bake in the oven for 30 minutes.

Salade façon césar
CAESAR SALAD WITH CHICKEN

Preheat the oven to 180°C (350°F/Gas 4).

Strip a chicken carcass to remove all of the flesh, then finely chop the leftover chicken.

To make the croutons, chop 1 garlic clove and dice 2 slices of sandwich bread. Combine the bread and garlic in a bowl and lay on a baking tray lined with baking paper. Bake in the oven until they dry out.

To make the vinaigrette, put 6 tablespoons of olive oil, 6 anchovies in oil and 1 tablespoon balsamic vinegar in a food processor, and blend until smooth.

Separate the leaves of 3 cos lettuces. Shave 50 g (1¾ oz) of parmesan cheese.

Combine the lettuce leaves with chicken pieces in a large bowl. Scatter over the croutons and parmesan shavings, then dress with the anchovy vinaigrette and garnish with tarragon sprigs.

Soupe de poulet façon thaïe
THAI CHICKEN SOUP

Strip a chicken carcass to remove all of the flesh, then finely chop the leftover chicken.

Peel and slice 3 onions and 3 leeks. Peel and dice 2 carrots.

Cover the chicken carcass in a large saucepan of water, then add the onion, leek and diced carrot. Simmer gently for 1 hour.

Remove the carcass, add the chopped chicken, 300 g (10½ oz) of fresh peas and 100 g (3½ oz) of peeled broad beans, and continue to cook for 15 minutes.

Add coriander (cilantro) sprigs and 150 ml (5 fl oz) of coconut cream. Season with salt and pepper.

Sandwich du dimanche soir
SUNDAY NIGHT TV SANDWICH

Carve the leftover meat of a lunchtime roast into thin slices.

Peel 1 red onion and slice into thin rings. Cut 3 tomatoes and 200 g (7 oz) of comté cheese into thin slices.

Brush 12 slices of a country-style loaf with olive oil. Place them under the griller and brown on just one side.

Put 2 tablespoons of mayonnaise, 1 tablespoon of tomato sauce (ketchup) and 1 teaspoon of worcestershire sauce into a small bowl and mix well. Spread the sauce onto the untoasted side of 6 slices of bread. Top with the meat, onion rings, tomato and cheese, then add a small spoonful of sauce on top. Cover with the other slice of bread.

Enjoy your program!

Œufs mimosa au poulet
CHICKEN STUFFED EGGS

Bring a large saucepan of lightly vinegared water to the boil.

Immerse 8 eggs, at room temperature, into the saucepan and cook for 10 minutes, then run them under cold water.

Finely chop leftover chicken meat.

Shell the eggs.

Halve 6 eggs and remove the yolks. Mash the egg yolks along with the other two whole eggs.

Peel and finely chop half a French shallot. Finely chop 1 bunch of chives. Combine the shallot, chives, chicken and mashed eggs and mix well with 80 ml (2½ fl oz) of mayonnaise. Season with salt and pepper.

Fill each egg half with the egg stuffing.

Spring

Summer

Winter

Autumn

Et avec tout ça?

(GARNITURES ET ACCOMPAGNEMENTS)

And with all this?
vegetables and side dishes

Petits pois à la française
FRENCH-STYLE GREEN PEAS

Chop 200 g (7 oz) piece of smoked streaky bacon into small pieces. Finely chop the heart of 1 lettuce and 6 bulb spring onions (scallions).

Heat 2 tablespoons of olive oil in a heavy-based saucepan. Add the onion and bacon and sauté over medium heat. Add 2 kg (4 lb 8 oz) of fresh peas, the lettuce, 1 bouquet garni and 200 ml (7 fl oz) of water. Cover and cook over low heat for 15 minutes, stirring regularly.

Add 50 g (1¾ oz) of butter to thicken the juices. Season with salt and pepper.

Courgettes à la menthe
MINTED ZUCCHINI

Halve lengthways 1 kg (2 lb 4 oz) zucchini (courgettes), then slice. Finely chop 2 garlic cloves. Peel and slice 1 bulb spring onion (scallion).

Strip the leaves from 1 bunch of mint and finely chop.

Heat 2 tablespoons of olive oil in a heavy-based saucepan. Add the garlic and onion and sauté over low heat without colouring them. Add the zucchini and mint, and sauté for 5 minutes: the zucchini should remain firm. Season with salt and pepper.

Jardinière de légumes printaniers
SPRING VEGETABLE MEDLEY

Scrape 1 bunch of new carrots and 1 bunch of baby turnips to remove the skin (don't use a peeler).

Slice the carrots and 2 zucchini. Cut the turnips into wedges. Peel and halve 3 bulb spring onions (scallions).

Pod 500 g (1 lb 2 oz) of fresh peas.

Heat 100 ml (3½ fl oz) of olive oil in a heavy-based saucepan. Add the carrot, onion and turnip and sauté over medium heat. Add 100 ml (3½ fl oz) of water and cook for 5 minutes.

Add the peas and cook for a further 5 minutes. Add the zucchini and continue to cook for 5 minutes: the vegetables will then be perfectly al dente. Season with fine sea salt.

Rattes aux herbes
KIPFLER POTATOES WITH HERBS

Thoroughly wash 1 kg (2 lb 4 oz) of kipfler potatoes, then rub clean with a dish cloth. Cut the potatoes in half.

Chop 1 bunch of chives.

Heat 50 g (1¾ oz) of butter in a large frying pan. Add the potato and brown over medium-high heat. Reduce the heat to low and continue to cook for 20 minutes.

Add the chives at the end of cooking and season with fine sea salt.

Tian provençal
PROVENÇALE VEGETABLE TIAN

Preheat the oven to 180°C (350°F/Gas 4).

Peel 2 onions and slice into rings. Slice 2 eggplants (aubergines), 2 zucchini (courgettes) and 2 tomatoes into rounds.

Chop 2 garlic cloves. Heat 100 ml (3½ fl oz) of olive oil in a frying pan and sauté the garlic over medium heat.

Oil a flameproof casserole dish with the garlic-infused oil.

Arrange the onion, eggplant, zucchini and tomato in the casserole dish, overlapping and wedging them in tightly.

Add a few rosemary sprigs and drizzle generously with olive oil. Season with fine sea salt, then bake in the oven for 1 hour.

Piperade
BASQUE VEGETABLE STEW

Finely chop 2 garlic cloves. Peel and finely chop 3 onions.

Slice 6 capsicums (peppers), yellow, green and red. Peel 3 very ripe tomatoes, retaining only the flesh.

Heat 100 ml (3½ fl oz) of olive oil in a heavy-based frying pan. Add the garlic, onion and capsicum and lightly brown over medium heat. Add the tomato flesh, 1 bay leaf and 1 tablespoon of brown sugar and combine well.

Add 3 slices of Basque ham (optional) and cook, covered, over low heat for 30 minutes. Season with salt (be careful as the salt from the ham is released during cooking) and pepper.

Ratatouille confite
SLOW-COOKED RATATOUILLE

Preheat the oven to 160°C (315°F/Gas 2–3).

Finely slice 4 garlic cloves. Peel and finely slice 3 onions.

Dice 2 eggplants (aubergines) and slice 2 red capsicums
(peppers).

Cut 4 tomatoes into wedges and dice 1 preserved lemon.

Slice 2 zucchini (courgettes) lengthways, then seed and dice.

Heat 150 ml (5 fl oz) of olive oil in a large flameproof casserole
dish. Add the garlic and onion and sauté over medium heat. Add
the eggplant and cook for 5 minutes. Add the capsicum, tomato,
lemon and zucchini and combine well. Add 2 bay leaves,
season with salt and pepper, then cook in the oven for 2 hours,
stirring regularly.

Bohémienne d'aubergines
EGGPLANT STEW

Peel and halve 6 French shallots. Chop 4 garlic cloves.

Dice 4 eggplants (aubergines).

Heat 100 ml (3½ fl oz) of olive oil in a saucepan, sauté
the garlic and shallot over medium heat. Add the
eggplant and sprinkle with mixed herbs. Stew over low
heat for 30 minutes. Season with salt and pepper.

Lentilles grassouillettes
CREAMY 'PUDGY' LENTILS

Peel and dice 3 carrots, 3 French shallots and 1 onion. Peel another onion and stud with 4 garlic cloves.

Put 250 g (9 oz) of lentils in a large saucepan and cover with cold water. Add the diced onion and carrot, the studded onion, 1 bouquet garni and 1 celery stalk. Bring to the boil and cook for 20 minutes. Strain and refresh immediately.

Heat 50 g (1¾ oz) of butter in a large heavy-based saucepan. Add the shallot and sauté over medium heat. Add 250 ml (9 fl oz/ 1 cup) of veal stock and 250 ml (9fl oz/1 cup) of cream. Reduce. Add the lentils to reheat. Season with salt and pepper.

Potimarron-châtaignes
PUMPKIN WITH CHESTNUTS

Chop 1 medium butternut pumpkin, seeds removed, into small cubes.

Peel and slice 2 onions.

Heat 150 ml (5 fl oz) of olive oil and 50 g (1¾ oz) of butter in a heavy-based frying pan. Add the onion and sauté over medium heat. Add the pumpkin, 1 teaspoon of ground turmeric and 1 teaspoon of rosemary leaves, and sauté over low heat for 15 minutes (the skin of the pumpkin should be soft).

Add 300 g (10½ oz) of chestnuts, roasted and peeled, and continue cooking for 10 minutes. Season with salt and pepper.

Cèpes confits
SLOW-COOKED CEP MUSHROOMS

Scrape the stems of 600 g (1 lb 5 oz) of fresh cep mushrooms
and rub them with a damp dish cloth.

Peel and slice 3 French shallots.

Melt 60 g (2¼ oz) of prosciutto fat in a flameproof casserole
dish. Add the shallot and 2 unpeeled garlic cloves. Arrange the
mushrooms on top, cover, and cook for 1 hour over low heat,
turning them at regular intervals. Season with salt and pepper.

The mushrooms will shrink to half their size and
the flavours and aromas will intensify.

Fruits et légumes d'automne
AUTUMN FRUIT AND VEGETABLES

Preheat the oven to 180°C (350°F/Gas 4).

Peel and slice 2 onions. Peel 3 pears and 3 firm-fleshed apples,
keeping the stems attached.

Zest and juice 1 orange.

Cut 2 fennel bulbs into thirds, and cook them in boiling
salted water for 10 minutes.

Arrange the pears, apples, onion and fennel in a flameproof
roasting tin. Pour over the orange juice, and add 80 g (2¾ oz)
of butter and 200 ml (7 fl oz) of white wine. Sprinkle with
1 tablespoon ground almonds and 1 tablespoon brown sugar.

Bake in the oven for 20 minutes, basting regularly with the
cooking juices.

Gratin dauphinois à l'ancienne
TRADITIONAL GRATIN DAUPHINOIS

Preheat the oven to 180°C (350°F/Gas 4).

Peel 1.5 kg (3 lb 5 oz) of potatoes, then slice them into thin rounds. Rinse the potatoes to remove all the starch, then dry them with a cloth.

Rub a flameproof roasting tin with a clove of garlic and fill with the potato slices.

Mix 1 teaspoon of nutmeg with 1 litre (35 fl oz/4 cups) of cream, season with salt and pepper. Pour the mixture over the potato and bake in the oven for 1 hour.

Gratin de pommes de terre boulanger
POTATO GRATIN BOULANGER

Preheat the oven to 180°C (350°F/Gas 4).

Peel 1.5 kg (3 lb 5 oz) of potatoes, 6 onions and 6 garlic cloves and slice all of them into thin rounds. Rinse the potatoes.

Butter a flameproof roasting tin. Make a layer of potato, add a few slices of onion and garlic, a bay leaf and a few small thyme sprigs. Repeat the process several times.

Cover the potato with 1 litre (35 fl oz/4 cups) of vegetable stock and bake in the oven for 45 minutes.

Pour any meat roasting juices over the gratin just before serving.

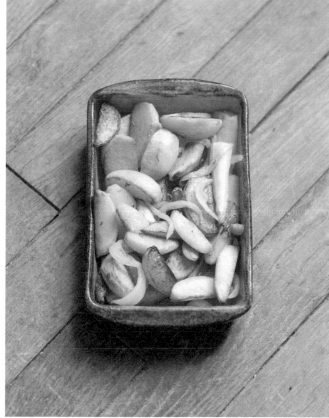

Gratin de cardons à la moelle
CARDOON GRATIN WITH MARROW

Cut the stalks of 1 bunch of cardoons in half lengthways.
Remove the stringy fibres. Slice each stalk diagonally and
cook in a saucepan of boiling water with the juice of 1 lemon
for 30 minutes.

Reduce the cooking liquid to 750 ml (26 fl oz/3 cups).

Preheat the oven to 180°C (350°F/Gas 4).

Melt 50 g (1¾ oz) of butter in a saucepan. Add 50 g (1¾ oz) of
plain (all-purpose) flour and cook over low heat for 2 minutes,
stirring. Add the reduced cooking liquid and 250 ml (9 fl oz/
1 cup) of cream, and cook for 5 minutes, stirring well. Season
with salt and pepper.

Place the cardoon in a flameproof roasting tin, cover with the
sauce and cook in the oven for 15 minutes. Top with 200 g (7 oz)
of thinly sliced marrow and place under the griller for 5 minutes.

Poêlée de légumes oubliés
SAUTÉ OF 'FORGOTTEN VEGETABLES'

Peel and cut into wedges 3 parsnips, 3 swedes (rutabagas)
and 6 jerusalem artichokes. Peel and slice 3 onions.

Cook the parsnip, swede and jerusalem artichoke separately
in boiling salted water for about 25 minutes: they should
remain firm.

Melt 50 g (1¾ oz) of butter in a frying pan with 150 ml
(5 fl oz) of olive oil. Add the onions and sauté them
over medium heat, then add the vegetables and sauté
for 5 minutes. Season with salt and pepper.

Index

TABLE OF CONTENTS

Published in 2009 by Murdoch Books Pty Limited
First published by Marabout (Hachette Livre) 2008

Murdoch Books Australia
Pier 8/9
23 Hickson Road
Millers Point NSW 2000
Phone: +61 (0) 2 8220 2000
Fax: +61 (0) 2 8220 2558
www.murdochbooks.com.au

Murdoch Books UK Limited
Erico House, 6th Floor
93–99 Upper Richmond Road
Putney, London SW15 2TG
Phone: +44 (0) 20 8785 5995
Fax: +44 (0) 20 8785 5985
www.murdochbooks.co.uk

Publisher: Jane Lawson
Editor: Sandra Loy
English translation: Melissa McMahon
Photography: Frédéric Lucano
Illustrations: Tabas
Production: Elizabeth Malcolm

Copyright © Marabout (Hachette Livre) 2008
Photography and illustrations © 2008

All rights reserved. No part of this publication may be reproduced,
stored in a retrieval system or transmitted in any form or by any means,
electronic, mechanical, photocopying, recording or otherwise, without
the prior written permission of the publisher.

National Library of Australia Cataloguing-in-Publication Data

Author: Reynaud, Stéphane.
Title: Rotis : roasts for every day of the week / Stéphane Reynaud.
ISBN: 9781741965377 (hbk.)
Notes: Includes index.
Subjects: Cookery. Roasting (Cookery)
Dewey Number: 641.71

A catalogue record for this book is available from the British Library.

PRINTED IN CHINA.

OVEN GUIDE: You may find cooking times vary depending on the oven
you are using. For fan-forced ovens, as a general rule, set the oven
temperature to 20°C (35°F) lower than indicated in the recipe.